Kanji Alchemy

700 Japanese Characters One Reading

Kanji Alchemy

700 Japanese Characters One Reading

Harry Nap

Copyright © 2024 Harry Nap
All rights reserved.
ISBN 978-0-9941965-2-1 Ingram PB
www.kanjialchemy.com

Contents

Introduction	IX
Chapter 1 Weeks 1 – 7	1
Chapter 2 Weeks 8 – 14	25
Chapter 3 Weeks 15 – 21	49
Chapter 4 Weeks 22 – 28	75
Chapter 5 Weeks 29 – 35	99
Multiple Readings Kanji	115
Chapter 6 Weeks 36 – 42	125
Chapter 7 Weeks 43 – 49	149
Chapter 8 Weeks 50 – 56	173
Chapter 9 Weeks 57 – 63	197
Chapter 10 Weeks 64 – 70	221
Chapter 11 Weeks 71 – 73	245
Wordlist One Character One Reading	255
Radicals	263

Acknowledgments

Jim Breen's Kanjidic compilation of 6,355 kanji as specified in the JIS X0208 1990 standard has been used as the main source for Kanji Alchemy. This publication has included material from the JMdict (EDICT, etc.) dictionary files in accordance with the license provisions of the Electronic Dictionaries Research Group. See http://www.csse.monash.edu.au/~jwb/edict.html and http://www.edrdg.org/.

The Appendix: Unicode/Alchemical Symbols that is part of Wiktionary has been used for the Alchemical Symbols in this text. https://en.wiktionary.org/wiki/Appendix:Unicode/Alchemical_Symbols

Illustrations were taken from the following Alchemical Texts
Michael Maier
Atalanta Fugiens (1617)
Edward Kelly
The Theatre of Terrestrial Astronomy (1676)
Basil Valentine
Azoth (1569)

Introduction

As students of Japanese are aware, simply trying to read a Japanese text can be a major undertaking requiring substantial investment of time and effort. Due to various reasons most Japanese characters (kanji) have two or more pronunciations and frequently different meanings as well. Although kanji often have a Sino-Chinese reading (on-yomi), a native Japanese reading (kun-yomi) and a reading for Japanese names (nanori), they on occasion only have one reading. This textbook is designed to highlight a range of nearly 700 characters that have **one** reading only.

The current Jouyou Kanji (regular-use kanji) list consists of 2136 characters so approximately one-third of these characters have a one-to-one relationship between sound and symbol. This, of course, greatly lessens the burden on memory and, if one starts learning these kanji from the beginning, considerably facilitates the whole study process.

The key to finding out which kanji have only one reading is by using Japanese websites rather than English websites. The difference is that on Japanese websites a filter is applied that alerts the reader that some readings are outside of the official Jouyou Kanji list. Western websites, by contrast, just show all the the listings. It follows that the life of a student of Japanese will be a great deal less complicated if these readings outside (外) of the official list are disregarded for the time being. The additional readings are genuine of course but can always be learned later when the need arises.

Following is an overview of the way in which these Japanese characters have been allocated.[1]

音 - on-yomi
訓 - kun-yomi
外 –outside of the Jouyou Kanji list

---

[1] The Japanese websites that were used are: https://dictionary.goo.ne.jp, https://www.kanjipedia.jp and https://ja.wiktionary.org.

One reading

| 感 カン 音 emotion; feeling |

More than one reading listed on western websites   **One reading listed on Japanese websites**

| 看 カン 音 + みる 訓 watch over | 看 カン 音 + (みる) 訓 **外** watch over |
| 観 カン 音 + みる + しめす 訓 outlook; look | 観 カン 音 + (みる + しめす) 訓 **外** look |

Multiple readings

| 肝 カン 音 + きも 訓 liver; nerve |
| 汗 カン 音 + あせ 訓 sweat; perspire |

It will be clear that '**One reading**' (no additional listings) and 'Multiple readings' are unambiguous. In the middle section みる+しめす are listed as being outside (外) of the Jouyou Kanji list on Japanese websites whereas that's not the case on western websites. In the case that a character is listed with (外), excluding a second reading like kun-yomi, it has been included in the 'one character one reading' list. The list of approximately 700 kanji with one reading used here has been entirely based on the output of Japanese websites.

The first part of the textbook covers about 700 'one character one reading' kanji followed by the second part that deals with the remaining Japanese characters that have multiple readings. Kanji are listed in the conventional Japanese order in the first as well as in the second part. Each chapter has seven sections or weeks and each week consists of seven days. The smallest unit or day has three characters that are arranged in a way to help memorisation. The meanings of these three characters are reflected in a '**recollection sentence**', essentially a memory aid to make it easier to learn and retain the characters.

In addition to the '**three-character**' design, **kanji compounds**, a combination of two or more characters, are an essential feature as well. Kanji with only on-yomi -like the 700 in the first part of this textbook- occasionally have a meaning by themselves but in general need to be combined with other characters to generate vocabulary. Although seemingly counter-intuitive, studying kanji as compounds of two or more Japanese characters, especially when dealing with on-yomi, makes much more sense. Treating kanji as part of vocabulary, rather than isolated single characters, is a more efficient method for reading texts later on. The same could be argued for characters with kun-yomi even if these single characters function as verbs, adjectives and nouns. When additional kanji are introduced to form compounds with one of the three main characters, that unit in fact represents six or more characters. An effort has been made not to repeat the same characters in the second part of the textbook.

At the end of each chapter, all the featured compounds are listed in order to be studied for revision. One week contains 21 main characters ($7 \times 3 = 21$) and one chapter consists of 7 weeks ($7 \times 21 = 147$). The number of characters exceeds 300 as additional kanji are used to generate vocabulary. Going over the **list of compounds** on a regular basis is a crucial part of kanji revision.

Kanji

The adoption of Chinese characters has proven to be the equivalent of a linguistic Procrustes bed in the case of Japanese. A highly inflected language like Japanese has a structural disadvantage, as kanji --Han characters-- are much better suited as a writing system for languages that are similar to Chinese. Vietnamese had considerably less problems in adopting Chinese characters because it is an isolating tonal language like Chinese. Words in isolating languages are not subject to change and therefore don't need to represent aspect or time. In order to reflect morphological change, Japanese developed its own syllabaries. (kana) Hiragana is used for grammatical particles and inflectional affixes. The other set of syllabic signs, katakana, is employed to write non-Japanese loanwords and many adverbs. As a general guide kanji are used to write most nouns, verbs and adjective bases. When early in the first millennium AD Japan adopted kanji, at that time having no script of its own, two main strategies were employed to accommodate the script to the language. Kanji were selected on the basis of meaning and in relation to the sound. This process can be represented in the following way.

| Meaning--3some, 3dent, 3iary, 3ce, 3d |
| Sound-----3angle, 3ceps, 3cycle |

The reading of kanji that relate to Japanese morphemes (the smallest semantic elements in a language) on the basis of meaning is referred to as kun-reading. The kanji was assigned a Japanese pronunciation, sometimes more than one, and chosen for the correspondence with its meaning in Chinese. Although there can be multiple readings for one kanji, it also happens that some have no kun-reading at all.
The kun-reading of 流れ星 is naga(re)boshi, meteor, falling star. The on-reading or Sino-Japanese pronunciation is an approximation of the Chinese pronunciation at the time when the kanji was introduced. At different times kanji from various parts of China were adopted, with the result that some kanji have more than one on-reading and also have different meanings. There are three distinct echoes depending on whether the word was borrowed in the sixth century, the eighth century, or early in the millennium. The on-reading of 流星 is ryuusei, meteor, falling star. As many Chinese loanwords found their way into Japanese, it was only natural to write Chinese words with Chinese characters. This created an intriguing "distortion effect" as new words were created with kanji based on an approximation of the Chinese pronunciation combined with semantically selected kanji that ignored pronunciation altogether. Sino-Japanese morphemes like these have been instrumental in enriching Japanese with an extensive layer of vocabulary. This process has been compared to the role of Arabic within Persian and Turkish or Latin within the European languages. Sino-Japanese words relate to concepts that either were not in existence in Japanese at that time or were deemed to be more refined than their native equivalent. They take the form of kanji compounds (two or more kanji) that generally follow the on-reading. Single isolated kanji usually have a kun-reading.

There are according to tradition six types of kanji that, although no longer studied because of the confusing nature of the definitions, are useful in the sense that they shed light on the structure of kanji. The first four categories refer to structural composition, the last two to usage.

The largest of the categories representing 85% of kanji, are the **"semantic-phonetic"** characters. Consisting of two components, the phonetic component refers to the (long obsolete) pronunciation of the character. In Japanese this is the on-reading. The semantic element indicates the meaning or context. In the passing of time the semantic context has frequently been subject to change, making the interpretation of a character in many cases rather confusing. Also, the distinction between phonetic and semantic elements of a character is ambiguous as phonetic elements frequently have semantic connotations as well. An example is mosquito (蚊) that combines 虫 insect with 文 BUN to give "insect that makes a BUN sound".[2]

Radicals are recurring features in kanji that are worth memorising because they provide some structure and (occasionally) meaning to the character. A radical in kanji first of all refers to the element that was chosen to classify the character for easy reference in a dictionary. 部首 (ぶしゅ) or "section head" contain characters with similar graphic components. Starting off initially with more than 500 radicals, the list was whittled down to 214 "indexing components" popularised later in a dictionary that became known as the Kangxi dictionary. (In Japanese known as the Kōki Jiten.) Radical is an unfortunate translation as the term is more appropriately applied to inflected languages which Chinese is not. In addition, radical refers to the "semantic component" in kanji as opposed to the phonetic component. The distinction between the two is not absolute as radicals sometimes also

---

[2] A fraction of modern characters consists of **"pictographs"**, characters that purpose to be a literal graphic representation of an object. Examples of this type include tree or moon. Ideographs or **logograms** also represent a small number of modern kanji. These "symbols" essentially express a simple abstract concept like up and down. A small number of modern kanji consists of **"ideographs"**, usually a combination of pictographs to present an overall meaning. An example is rest, made from tree and person. **"Derivative characters"** or characters with borrowed meaning and pronunciation is a rather vague category. As the majority of characters have undergone some change of meaning, this particular classification is not so relevant. Sen used to mean divination but now has acquired a major meaning of occupy, replacing a more complex character with the same pronunciation. **"Phonetic loan characters"** are employed for their sound value to represent other but unrelated but homophonous morphemes. An example is lai "barley" in Chinese for lai "come". Kokuji **"Made in Japan"** characters are sometimes treated as a seventh category. The number in modern kanji is small. The most famous example is hataraku that combines person" radical with "movement" to create "work". The character has been adopted into written Chinese in the twentieth century.

xiii

play a phonetic role and phonetic elements occasionally have semantic connotations as well.

Radicals within characters may appear in seven positions.

かんむ	top kanji radical	(艹 grass)	花 若 苦
へん	left-side radical	(土 earth)	地 坂 城
つくり	right-side radical	(彡 three)	形 影 彫
たれ	radical top-left position	(广 cliff)	広 店 麻
あし	bottom kanji radical	(儿 legs)	先 兄 光
にょう	radical bottom-left position	(辶 road)	近 道 送
かまえ	radical enclosed position	(門 gate)	聞 閉 開

Given the fact that radicals feature extensively in kanji, a list of the most frequent radicals has been provided in the Appendix.

How to Use This Text

Both one-reading characters and kanji with multiple readings use the same structure that introduces three new kanji per unit. The main difference will be that the kanji with a single reading will be easier to memorise. This is what it looks like from the second week (2) and the second day (b).

| △ | 衛 | 宇 | 英 |
| 2 b | エイ | ウ | エイ |

Hygiene is close to Ecstasy as the Anglo-Saxons say.

The 'recollection sentence' refers to the meaning of the kanji and this is reflected through the use of capitals. '*Hygiene is close to Ecstasy as the Anglo-Saxons say.*' The sentence alludes to the meaning of the Japanese characters and should not be taken too literally. It follows that the sentence could point to a noun, adjective, adverb or even a synonym. As mentioned previously, the 'recollection sentence' is only a memory aid and the most important activity is to make the connection between the single character, the reading, the meaning and the kanji compound.

In this case there is no difference between the listings of 衛, 宇 and 英 as hygiene, ecstasy and Anglo-Saxon are the same as their compounds: 衛生 hygiene, 宇頂天 ecstasy and 独英.

The first table (above) shows three new kanji followed by a 'recollection sentence' that refers to the meanings of the characters. The second table (below) displays the single characters and the additional characters used to generate compounds.

衛	エイ	guard, protect	衛
衛生	えいせい	hygiene	2 b
生	セイ、ショウ、いきる	life, birth, grow	2 b
宇	ウ	eaves, roof, heaven	宇
宇頂天	うちょうてん	ecstasy	2 b
頂	チョウ、いただく	receive, top, crown	2 b
天	テン、あめ、あま	heaven, sky	2 b
英	エイ	superior, England	英
独	ドク、ひとり	alone, Germany	2 b
独英	どくえい	Anglo-Saxon	2 b

As mentioned previously, when studying kanji the suggested method is to focus on the compounds first and then to parse it's members -the addional Japanese characters- afterwards. In the case of 2 b that means that when seeing the recollection sentence featuring hygiene, ecstasy and Anglo-Saxon, the Japanese translation えいせい、うちょうてん plus どくえい should be the basis from which everything else follows. When seeing new material for the first time the second table must be studied in the usual way but when it comes to revision, it would be best to try to disregard the second table and to work out independently the corresponding Japanese vocabulary. Half of the word is already given which makes it easier. (In the second part with mutliple readings, on-yomi and kun-yomi have been omitted in the first table.) Each chapter ends with a list of 147 compounds exceeding 300 kanji that have been used in those seven weeks. Revision of the compound list should become a regular feature when studying kanji. This is what it looks like.

	1	2	3	4	5	6	7
a	亜欧	署員	憶測	侵害	且つ又	生還	儀式
	挨拶	婚姻	甲乙丙	貝殻	芝刈り機	勇敢	模擬
	愛国	音韻	恩返し	天涯	株価	悪循環	犠牲
b	案出	**衛生**	学科	弾劾	寛容	召喚	閑却
	取り扱い	**宇頂天**	蚊柱	該当	韓国	缶切り	残菊
	圧伏	**独英**	貨幣	憤慨	看護	勘定	喫茶店

Note that the table has a vertical flow and that the letter g (day seven) would be the end point. Of the seven weeks, only a and b are represented. 2 b is here in bold print.

It is true that, other than suggesting that memorising a number of radicals would be beneficial, no other suggestions have been given to aid memorisation of kanji as a graphic character. In other volumes of the Kanji Alchemy series, the emphasis was strongly on highlighting graphic similarities of the characters as a means to kanji recognition.[3] An almost perfect example can be seen in 67 b where not only the form but even the on-yomi are the same. The only difference is in the kun-yomi and semantics. *'Recruitment for the Dear Graveyard'* is the recollection sentence.

	募	慕	墓
67 b	♎	♉	♎

---

3 Kanji Alchemy: A Strategy for Reading Japanese Characters, Kanji Alchemy-Back to the Roots Learning
Japanese Characters with a Radical Focus.

xvi

The radicals 力 心 土 (strength, heart and earth) provide the semantics that in this case actually make sense. Unfortunately, this is an exception and generally speaking radicals don't offer that much information.

In this textbook no further strategies such as character analysis, etymology of the character, or mnemonics will be offered. An important reason for being careful with using techniques such as mnemonics is that the 'scaffolding' of the memorisation system can take prevalence over the material that is being studied in the first place. Only remembering '*Hygiene is close to Ecstasy as the Anglo-Saxons say.*' without being able to at least pronounce the corresponding Japanese vocabulary and being able to work out the reading of one character, would be a waste of time. In the not too distant past there were no elaborate systems on how to memorise kanji. So it will be, in other words, up to the student to devise ways on how to commit the graphic form of the character to memory. In any event, it is crucial to map readings to the character and to be able to pronounce it. To a large extent, this challenge has been made less cumbersome as far as 700 kanji with only one reading are concerned.[4] For additional information, please refer to https://kanjialchemy.com.

---

[4] Works consulted in the course of creating this textbook.
Coulmas, Florian (1981), Ueber Schrift, Suhrkamp Taschenbuch Wissenschaft
DeFrancis, John (1984), Chinese Language: Fact and Fantasy, University of Hawaii Press
Henshall, Kenneth G. (1995), A Guide to Remembering Japanese Characters, Tuttle
O'Neill, P.G. (1973), Essential Kanji, Weatherhill
Ostler, Nicholas (2006), Empires of the World, Harper Perennial.

CHAPTER 1
Weeks 1 – 7

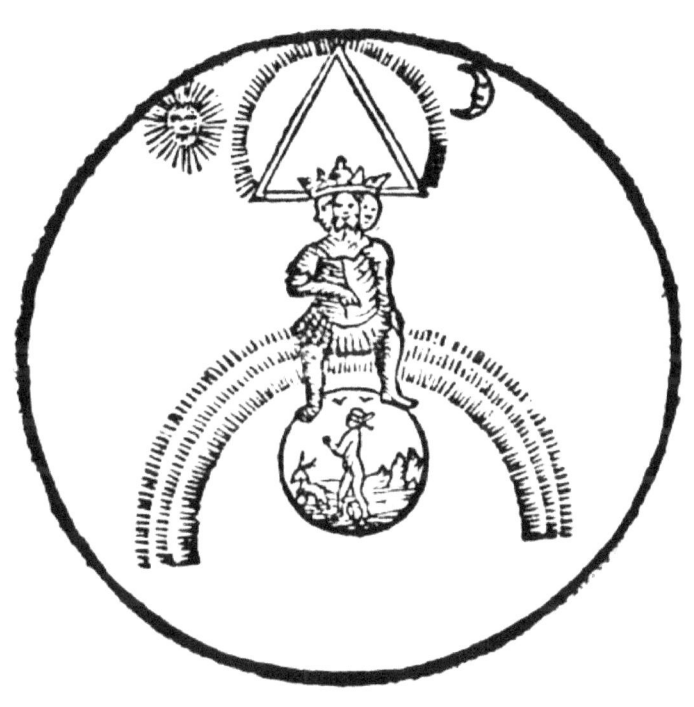

△	亜	挨	愛
1 a	ア	アイ	アイ

Eurasian Greetings and continental Patriotism.

亜	ア	next, sub-, Asia	亜
亜欧	あおう	Asia and Europe; Eurasia	1 a
欧	オウ	Europe, eu-	1 a
挨	アイ	push open	挨
挨拶	あいさつ	greetings	1 a
拶	サツ	imminent	1 a
愛	アイ	love	愛
愛国	あいこく	patriotism	1 a
国	コク、くに	country, region	1 a

△	案	扱	圧
1 b	アン	あつかう	アツ

An Invention for Handling Pressure.

案	アン	plan	案
案出	あんしゅつ	contrivance; invention	1 b
出	シュツ、スイ、でる	emerge, put out	1 b
扱	あつかう	treat, handle, thresh	扱
取り扱い	とりあつかい	handling	1 b
取	シュ、とる	take control	1 b
圧	アツ	pressure	圧
圧伏	あっく	overpower; subdue	1 b
伏	フク、ふせる	prostrated, bend down	1 b

△	維	意	椅
1 c	イ	イ	イ

Fasten your Will to the Chair.

維	イ	fasten, rope, support	維
維持	いじ	upkeep	1 c
持	ジ、もつ	hold, maintain	1 c
意	イ	mind, will	意
意志	いし	will	1 c
志	シ、こころざす	will, intent	1 c
椅	イ	chair	椅
椅子	いす	chair	1 c
子	シ、ス、こ	child	1 c

△	委	医	胃
1 d	イ	イ	イ

Commit your Stomach to a Doctor.

委	イ	committee, entrust to	委
委託	いたく	commission	1 d
託	タク	entrust, commit	1 d
医	イ	doctor	医
医者	はいしゃ	doctor	1 d
者	シャ、もの	person	1 d
胃	イ	stomach	胃
胃袋	いぶくろ	stomach	1 d
袋	タイ、ふくろ	bag, pouch	1 d

△	以	尉	緯
1 e	イ	イ	イ

With a Military Rank there is some Latitude.

以	イ	means, through, because	以
以内	いない	within	1 e
内	ナイ、ダイ、うち	inside	1 e
尉	イ	military rank	尉
小尉	しょい	ensign	1 e

小	ショウ、ちいさい、こ	small	1 e
緯	イ	horizontal, weft	緯
緯度	いど	latitude	1 e
度	ド、ト、タク、たび	degree, times	1 e

△	為	域	威
1 f	イ	イキ	イ

What to Do with the Limits of Authority?

為	イ	do, purpose	為
行為	こうい	action, act	1 f
行	コウ、ギョウ、いく	go, conduct, column	1 f
域	イキ	area, limits	域
領域	りょういき	domain	1 f
領	リョウ	control, chief, territory	1 f
威	イ	authority, threaten	威
威力	いりょく	authority,	1 f
力	リョク、リキ、ちから	strength, effort	1 f

△	壱	芋	院
1 g	イチ	いも	イン

One Potato for each member of the Lower House.

壱	イチ	one	壱
壱万円	いちまんえん	10,000 Yen	1 g
万	マン、バン	ten thousand, myriad	1 g
円	エン、まるい	round, yen	1 g
芋	いも	potato	芋
里芋	さといも	taro	1 g
里	リ、さと	village, league	1 g
院	イン	institute	院
衆院	しゅういん	Lower House of the Diet	1 g
衆	シュウ、シュ	multitude, populace	1 g

△	員	姻	韻
2 a	イン	イン	イン

The Official Married the Phonemes.

員	イン	member, official	員
署員	しょいん	official	2 a
署	ショ	government, office, sign	2 a
姻	イン	marriage	姻
婚姻	こんいん	marriage	2 a
婚	コン	marriage	2 a
韻	イン	rhyme, tone	韻
音韻	おんいん	phoneme	2 a
音	オン、イン、おと、ね	sound	2 a

△	衛	宇	英
2 b	エイ	ウ	エイ

Hygiene is close to Ecstasy as the Anglo-Saxons say.

衛	エイ	guard, protect	衛
衛生	えいせい	hygiene	2 b
生	セイ、ショウ、いきる	life, birth, grow	2 b
宇	ウ	eaves, roof, heaven	宇
宇頂天	うちょうてん	ecstasy	2 b
頂	チョウ、いただく	receive, top, crown	2 b
天	テン、あめ、あま	heaven, sky	2 b
英	エイ	superior, England	英
独	ドク、ひとり	alone, Germany	2 b
独英	どくえい	Anglo-Saxon	2 b

△	液	駅	悦
2 c	エキ	エキ	エツ

Every Droplet from Each Station is a Joyful event.

液	エキ	liquid	液
液滴	えきてき	droplet	2 c
滴	テキ、しずく、したたる	drop, drip	2 c
駅	エキ	station	駅
各駅	かくえき	each station	2 c
各	カク、おのおの	each	2 c
悦	エツ	joy	悦
悦楽	えつらく	enjoyment	2 c
楽	ガク、ラク、たのしい	pleasure, music	2 c

△	閲	演	謁
2 d	エツ	エン	エツ

Harsh Censorship of the Play before an Audience.

閲	エツ	inspection	閲
検閲	けんえつ	censorship	2 d
検	ケン	investigate	2 d
演	エン	performance, play	演
演芸会	えんげいかい	an entertainment, variety show	2 d
芸	ゲイ	art, skill, plant	2 d
会	カイ、エ、あう	meet	2 d
謁	エツ	audience (with ruler)	謁
拝謁	はいえつ	audience	2 d
拝	ハイ、おがむ	worship, respectful	2 d

△	王	宴	援
2 e	オウ	エン	エン

The Royal Banquet brought Relief.

王	オウ	king	王
王妃	おうひ	queen, princess	2 e
妃	ヒ	queen, princess	2 e

宴	エン	banquet	宴
宴会	えんかい	party; banquet	2 e
会	カイ、エ、あう	meet	2 e
援	エン	help	援
救援	きゅうえん	relief, rescue	2 e
救	キュウ、すくう	rescue, redeem	2 e

△	往	翁	応
2 f	オウ	オウ	オウ

In Times Past Revered Old Mr. Kaneda had a heated Exchange.

往	オウ	go, gone, past	往
往時	おうじ	times past	2 f
時	ジ、とき	time	2 f
翁	オウ	old man, venerable	翁
金田翁	かねだおう	revered old Mr. Kaneda	2 f
金	キン、コン、かね	gold, money, metal	2 f
田	デン、た	rice field	2 f
応	オウ	respond, react	応
応酬	おうしゅう	exchange; reply; riposte	2 f
酬	シュウ	reward, toast, reply	2 f

△	欧	央	億
2 g	オウ	オウ	オク

The European Industrial Center lost Hundreds of Millions.

欧	オウ	Europe, eu-	欧
欧州	おうしゅう	Europe	2 g
州	シュウ、す	state, province	2 g
央	オウ	center	央
震央	しんおう	epicenter	2 g
震	シン、ふるう	shake, tremble	2 g
億	オク	hundred million	億

億兆	おくちょう	the people; the masses	2 g
兆	チョウ、きざす	sign, omen, trillion	2 g

▽	憶	乙	恩
3 a	オク	オツ	オン

Speculation on the ABC scheme will not do you any Favours.

憶	オク	think, remember	憶
憶測	おくそく	speculation	3 a
測	ソク、はかる	measure, fathom	3 a
乙	オツ	odd, b, 2nd, stylish	乙
甲乙丙	こう/おつ/へい	abc/123	3 a
甲	コウ、カン	shell, armour, high, 1st, a	3 a
丙	ヘイ	c, 3rd	3 a
恩	オン	favour, kindness	恩
恩返し	おんがえし	return favour	3 a
返	ヘン、かえす	return	3 a

▽	科	蚊	貨
3 b	カ	カ	カ

A Course on Mosquito Swarms will cost Money.

科	カ	course, section	科
学科	がっか	school subjects	3 b
学	ガク、まな-ぶ	study	3 b
蚊	カ	mosquito	蚊
蚊柱	かばしら	mosquito swarm	3 b
柱	チュウ、はしら	column, pillar	3 b
貨	カ	goods, money	貨
貨幣	かへい	coin, money	3 b
幣	ヘイ	offering, money	3 b

▽	可	課	菓
3 c	カ	カ	カ

It's not hard to get Approval from Section Head Candy Floss.

可	カ	approve, can, should	可
可決	かけつ	approval	3 c
決	ケツ、きめる、きまる	decide, settle, collapse	3 c
課	カ	section, lesson, levy	課
課長	かちょう	section head	3 c
長	チョウ、なが-い	long, senior	3 c
菓	カ	fruit, cake	菓
綿菓子	わたがし	candy floss	3 c
綿	メン、わた	cotton, cotton wool	3 c
子	シ、ス、こ	child	3 c

▽	寡	禍	佳
3 d	カ	カ	カ

Widow Calamity was Beautiful but not Good.

寡	カ	few, minimum, widow	寡
寡婦	かふ	widow	3 d
婦	フ	woman, wife	3 d
禍	カ	calamity	禍
禍根	かこん	root of evil	3 d
根	コン、ね	root, base	3 d
佳	カ	beautiful, good	佳
絶佳	ぜっか	superb	3 d
絶	ゼツ、たえる、たやす	cease, sever, end	3 d

▽	餓	雅	賀
3 e	ガ	ガ	ガ

Starved for Elegant Celebrations.

餓	ガ		starve	餓
餓鬼	がき		hungry imp, brat	3 e
鬼	キ、おに		devil, demon, ghost	3 e
雅	ガ		elegance, 'taste'	雅
優雅	ゆうが		elegance	3 e
優	ユウ、やさしい、すぐれる		superior, actor	3 e
賀	ガ		congratulations	賀
祝賀	しゅくが		celebrate	3 e
祝	シュク、シュウ、いわう		celebration	3 e

▽	介	楷	界
3 f	カイ	カイ	カイ

Introducing Square Characters from the Nether World.

介	カイ	mediate, shell	介
紹介	しょうかい	introduction	3 f
紹	ショウ	introduce, inherit	3 f
楷	カイ	square character style; correctness	楷
楷書	かいしょ	non-cursive kanji	3 f
書	ショ、かく	write	3 f
界	カイ	area, boundary	界
鬼界	きかい	nether world	3 f
鬼	キ、おに	devil, demon, ghost	3 f

▽	階	械	械
3 g	カイ	カイ	カイ

A carefully Graded Kidnapping Device.

階	カイ	story, grade, step	階
階段	かいだん	stairs	3 g
段	ダン	step, grade	3 g
拐	カイ	deceive, kidnap, bend	械
誘拐	ゆうかい	abduction; kidnapping	3 g

誘	ユウ、さそう	invite, tempt, lead	3 g
械	カイ	device	械
器械	きかい	apparatus	3 g
器	キ、うつわ	vessel, utensil, skill	3 g

▽	害	貝	涯
4 a	ガイ	かい	ガイ

Invading Shellfish on the Horizon.

害	ガイ	harm, damage	害
侵害	しんがい	violation	4 a
侵	シン、おかす	invade, violate	4 a
貝	かい	shellfish	貝
貝殻	かいがら	sea shell	4 a
殻	カク、から	shell, husk, crust	4 a
涯	ガイ	shore, edge	涯
天涯	てんがい	horizon	4 a
天	テン、あめ、あま	heaven, sky	4 a

▽	劾	該	慨
4 b	ガイ	ガイ	ガイ

Investigate Relevant Indignation.

劾	ガイ	investigate (wrong doing)	劾
弾劾	だんがい	impeachment	4 b
弾	ダン、ひく、はずむ	bullet, spring, play	4 b
該	ガイ	relevance, the said-	該
該当	がいとう	relevance	4 b
当	トウ、あたる、あてる	apply, hit, mark, this	4 b
慨	ガイ	lament, deplore	慨
憤慨	ふんがい	indignation	4 b
憤	フン、いきどおる	indignant, angry	4 b

▽	概	垣	較
4 c	ガイ	かき	カク

A General Look over the fence is without Comparison.

概	ガイ	roughly, in general	概
概略	がいりゃく	outline	4 c
略	リャク	abbreviate, outline	4 c
垣	かき	fence, hedge	垣
垣間見る	かいまみる*	peep	4 c
間	カン、ケン、あいだ、ま	space, gap	4 c
見	ケン、み-る、みえる	look, see, show	4 c
較	カク	comparison	較
比較	ひかく	comparison	4 c
比	ヒ、くらべる	compare, ratio	4 c

▽	嚇	拡	閣
4 d	カク	カク	カク

A Threatening Spread of honest conduct in the Cabinet.

嚇	カク	threaten, menace	嚇
威嚇	いかく	threat, intimidation	4 d
威	イ	authority, threaten	4 d
拡	カク	spread	拡
拡大	かくだい	magnification	4 d
大	ダイ、タイ、おおきい	big	4 d
閣	カク	cabinet, chamber	閣
内閣	ないかく	cabinet	4 d
内	ナイ、ダイ、うち	inside	4 d

▽	郭	核	穫
4 e	カク	カク	カク

Outlines of a Nuclear Harvest.

郭	カク	quarter, enclosure	郭
輪郭	りんかく	outlines	4 e
輪	リン、わ	wheel, hoop	4 e
核	カク	core, nucleus, nuclear	核
核兵器	かくへいき	nuclear weapon	4 e
兵	ヘイ、ヒョウ	soldier	4 e
器	キ、うつわ	vessel, utensil, skill	4 e
穫	カク	harvest	穫
収穫	しゅうかく	harvest	4 e
収	シュウ、おさめる	obtain, store, supply	4 e

| ▽ | 活 | 潟 | 括 |
| 4 f | カツ | かた | カツ |

Life on a Tidal Flat, it is a Wrap.

活	カツ	activity, life	活
生活	せいかつ	life	4 f
生	セイ、ショウ、いきる	life, birth, grow	4 f
潟	かた	beach, lagoon	潟
干潟	ひがた	tidal flat, dry beach	4 f
干	カン、ほ-す、ひ-る	dry, defense	4 f
括	カツ	bind, wrap, fasten	括
括弧	かっこ	parentheses	4 f
弧	コ	arc, arch, bow	4 f

| ▽ | 轄 | 褐 | 喝 |
| 4 g | カツ | カツ | カツ |

Controlling Mr Brown loudly Shouted "catch you".

轄	カツ	control, linchpin	轄
管轄	かんかつ	jurisdiction	4 g
管	カン、くだ	pipe, control	4 g
褐	カツ	brown, coarse cloth	褐

褐色	かっしょく	brown	4 g
色	ショク、シキ、いろ	colour, sensuality	4 g
喝	カツ	shout, scold	喝
喝采	かっさい	applause; ovation; cheers	4 g
采	サイ、とる	dice; form; take; coloring	4 g

▽	且	刈	株
5 a	かつ	かる	かぶ

And Furthermore, Cut those Shares I say.

且	かつ	furthermore, besides	且
且つ又	かつまた	moreover	5 a
又	また	or again	5 a
刈	かる	reap, cut, shear	刈
芝刈り機	しばかりき	lawn mower	5 a
芝	しば	lawn, turf	5 a
機	キ、はた	loom, device, occasion	5 a
株	かぶ	stock, share, stump	株
株価	かぶか	stock prices	5 a
価	カ、あたい	price, value, worth	5 a

▽	寛	韓	看
5 b	カン	カン	カン

Broadminded Korean home Nursing.

寛	カン	magnanimous, relax	寛
寛容	かんよう	tolerance	5 b
容	ヨウ	contain, looks	5 b
韓	カン	Korea	韓
韓国	かんこく	South Korea	5 b
国	コク、くに	country, region	5 b
看	カン	watch	看
看護	かんご	nursing, nurse	5 b

護	ゴ	defend, protect	5 b

▽	感	簡	閑
5 c	カン	カン	カン

Feelings of Simple Tranquility.

感	カン	feeling	感
感情	かんじょう	feeling	5 c
情	ジョウ、セイ、なさけ	feeling, pity, fact	5 c
簡	カン	simple, brief	簡
簡素	かんそな	simplicity; plain	5 c
素	ソ、ス	element, base, bare	5 c
閑	カン	leasure, quiet	閑
閑寂	かんじゃく	quiet, tranquility	5 c
寂	ジャク、セキ、さびしい	quiet, lonely	5 c

▽	刊	完	憾
5 d	カン	カン	カン

Final Issue of Flawless Regret.

刊	カン	publish, engrave	刊
終刊号	しゅうかんごう	last issue of a publication	5 d
終	シュウ、おわる	end, finish	5 d
号	ゴウ	number, call, sign	5 d
完	カン	complete	完
完璧	かんぺき	perfect; flawless	5 d
璧	ヘキ たま	sphere; ball	5 d
憾	カン	regret	憾
遺憾な	いかん な	regrettable	5 d
遺	イ、ユイ	leave, bequeath, lose	5 d

▽	官	款	館
5 e	カン	カン	カン

The Official was on Loan from the Museum.

官	カン	government, official	官
官司	かんし	government office	5 e
司	シ	administer, official	5 e
款	カン	friendship, clause, engrave	款
借款	しゃっかん	loan, credit	5 e
借	シャク、かりる	borrow, rent	5 e
館	カン	large building, hall	館
博物館	はくぶつかん	museum	5 e
博	ハク、バク	extensive, spread, gain	5 e
物	ブツ、モツ、もの	thing	5 e

▽	観	漢	棺
5 f	カン	カン	カン

As Optimistic as a Kanji Coffin.

観	カン	watch, observe	観
楽観的	らっかんてき	optimistic	5 f
楽	ガク、ラク、たのしい	pleasure, music	5 f
的	テキ、まと	target, like, adj. suffix	5 f
漢	カン	Han China, man	漢
漢字	かんじ	kanji	5 f
字	ジ、あざ	letter, symbol	5 f
棺	カン	coffin	棺
棺おけ	かんおけ	coffin, casket	5 f

▽	歓	監	艦
5 g	カン	カン	カン

It was a Pleasure to Observe the Cutter called Kan.

歓	カン	rejoice, merry	歓
歓楽	かんらく	pleasure	5 g

楽	ガク、ラク、たのしい	pleasure, music	5 g
監	カン	supervise, watch	監
監視	かんし	observation	5 g
視	シ	see, look, regard	5 g
艦	カン	warship	艦
軍艦	ぐんかん	warship	5 g
軍	グン	military, army	5 g

⌐R	還	敢	環
6 a	カン	カン	カン

Surviving a Tragic and Vicious Circle.

還	カン	return	還
生還	せいかん	surviving	6 a
生	セイ、ショウ、いきる	life, birth, grow	6 a
敢	カン	daring, tragic	敢
勇敢	ゆうかん	bravery, valour	6 a
勇	ユウ、いさむ	courage	6 a
環	カン	ring, circle	環
悪循環	あくじゅんかん	vicious circle	6 a
悪	アク、オ、わるい	bad, hate	6 a
循	ジュン	follow	6 a

⌐R	喚	缶	勘
6 b	カン	カン	カン

Summon the Can Opener to present the Bill.

喚	カン	shout, yell	喚
召喚	しょうかん	summons	6 b
召	ショウ、め-す	summon, partake	6 b
缶	カン	can, boiler	缶
缶切り	かんきり	can opener	6 b
切	セツ、サイ、きる	cut	6 b

勘	カン		endure, investigate	勘
勘定	かんじょう		bill, account	6 b
定	テイ、ジョウ、さだめる		fix, establish	6 b

℞	紀	軌	頑
6 c	キ	キ	ガン

Epochal Examplary Stubborness.

紀	キ		chronicle, start	紀
紀元	きげん		epoch, era	6 c
元	ゲン、ガン、もと		originally, source	6 c
軌	キ		track, rut, way	軌
軌範	きはん		model, example	6 c
範	ハン		model, norm, limits	6 c
頑	ガン		stubborn	頑
頑張る	がんばる		persevere	6 c
張	チョウ、はる		stretch	6 c

℞	揮	奇	騎
6 d	キ	キ	キ

Commanding a Curious Cavalry.

揮	キ		wield, shake, command	揮
指揮	しき		command	6 d
指	シ、ゆび、さす		finger, point	6 d
奇	キ		strange, odd	奇
珍奇	ちんき		strange, rare, curious	6 d
珍	チン、めずらしい		rare, curious	6 d
騎	キ		rider	騎
騎兵	きへい		cavalry	6 d
兵	ヘイ、ヒョウ		soldier	6 d

℞	棄	汽	棋

6 e	キ	キ	キ

Abstain from Steamy Chess.

棄	キ	abandon, renounce	棄
棄権	きけん	abstention	6 e
権	ケン、ゴン	right, authority, balance	6 e
汽	キ	steam	汽
汽笛	きてき	steam whistle	6 e
笛	テキ、ふえ	flute, whistle	6 e
棋	キ	chess	棋
将棋	しょうぎ	chess	6 e
将	ショウ	command, about to	6 e

⌂	季	規	希
6 f	キ	キ	キ

The Season for Regulated Desires.

季	キ	season	季
季候	きこう	climate	6 f
候	コウ、そうろう	weather, sign, ask, polite suf.	6 f
規	キ	standard, measure	規
規制	きせい	regulation, control	6 f
制	セイ	system, control	6 f
希	キ	desire, hope for, rare	希
希求	ききゅう	desire	6 f
求	キュウ、もとめる	request, seek	6 f

⌂	岐	議	義
6 g	キ	ギ	ギ

A Fork for Discussions and a spoon for Significance.

岐	キ	fork	岐

岐路	きろ	forked road	6 g
路	ロ、じ	road, route	6 g
議	ギ	discussion	議
議論	ぎろん	discussion	6 g
論	ロン	argument, opinion	6 g
義	ギ	righteousness	義
意義	いぎ	significance	6 g
意	イ	mind, thought, will	6 g

ꝗ	儀	擬	犠
7 a	ギ	ギ	ギ

The Ceremonial Imitation of a Sacrifice.

儀	ギ	ceremony, rule, case	儀
儀式	ぎしき	ceremony	7 a
式	シキ	ceremony, form	7 a
擬	ギ	imitate, model	擬
模擬	もぎ	imitation	7 a
模	モ、ボ	copy, model, mold	7 a
犠	ギ	sacrifice	犠
犠牲	ぎせい	sacrifice	7 a
牲	セイ	sacrifice	7 a

ꝗ	却	菊	喫
7 b	キャク	キク	キツ

He was Ignored at the Late Chrysanthemums Café.

却	キャク	(on the) contrary	却
閑却	かんきゃく	negligence; disregard	7 b
閑	カン	leasure, quiet	7 b
菊	キク	chrysanthemum	菊
残菊	ざんぎく	late chrysanthemums	7 b
残	ザン、のこる、のこす	leave, cruel, harm	7 b

喫	キツ	ingest, receive	喫
喫茶店	きっさてん	café	7 b
茶	チャ、サ	tea	7 b
店	テン、みせ	store, premises	7 b

㍿	旧	級	給
7 c	キュウ	キュウ	キュウ

Old Style Classmates: they do not Supply them like that anymore.

旧	キュウ	old, past	旧
旧式	きゅうしき	old style	7 c
式	シキ	ceremony, form	7 c
級	キュウ	rank, grade	級
同級生	どうきゅうせい	classmate	7 c
同	ドウ、おなじ	same	7 c
生	セイ、ショウ、いきる	life, birth, grow	7 c
給	キュウ	supply, bestow	給
供給	きょうきゅう	supply	7 c
供	キョウ、ク、そなえる、とも	offer, attendant	7 c

㍿	糾	巨	距
7 d	キュウ	キョ	キョ

Examen the Giant from a Distance.

糾	キュウ	entwine, examine	糾
糾明	きゅうめい	examination	7 d
明	メイ、ミョウ、あかるい	clear, open, bright	7 d
巨	キョ	huge, giant	巨
巨人	きょじん	giant	7 d
人	ジン、ニン、ひと	person	7 d
距	キョ	distance, cockspur	距
距離	きょり	distance	7 d
離	リ、はなれる、はなす	separate, leave	7 d

㋕	協	享	況
7 e	キョウ	キョウ	キョウ

The Association of Receivers demands better Conditions.

協	キョウ	cooperate	協
協会	きょうかい	association; society	7 e
会	カイ、エ、あう	meet	7 e
享	キョウ	receive, have	享
享受	きょうじゅ	enjoyment (freedom etc.)	7 e
受	ジュ、うける、うかる	receive	7 e
況	キョウ	more so, situation	況
状況	じょうきょう	situation	7 e
状	ジョウ	condition, letter	7 e

㋕	局	凶	峡
7 f	キョク	キョウ	キョウ

No Mail in the Disaster Straits.

局	キョク	office, section, end	局
郵便局	ゆうびんきょく	post office	7 f
郵	ユウ	mail, relay station	7 f
便	ベン、ビン、たより	convenience, mail	7 f
凶	キョウ	bad luck, disaster	凶
凶悪	きょうあくな	atrocious	7 f
悪	アク、オ、わるい	bad, hate	7 f
峡	キョウ	ravine, gorge	峡
海峡	かいきょう	straits	7 f
海	カイ、うみ	sea	7 f

㋕	斤	菌	均
7 g	キン	キン	キン

Weighty Fungi tip the Balance.

斤	キン	ax, weight	斤
斤目	きんめ	weight	7 g
目	モク、ボク、め、ま	eye, ordinal, suffix	7 g
菌	キン	fungus, bacteria	菌
殺菌	さっきん	steralize, disinfect	7 g
殺	サツ、サイ、セツ、ころす	kill	7 g
均	キン	level	均
均衡	きんこう	balance	7 g
衡	コウ	scales, yoke	7 g

Kanji Alchemy

	1	2	3	4	5	6	7
a	亜欧	署員	憶測	侵害	且つ又	生還	儀式
	挨拶	婚姻	甲乙丙	貝殻	芝刈り機	勇敢	模擬
	愛国	音韻	恩返し	天涯	株価	悪循環	犠牲
b	案出	衛生	学科	弾劾	寛容	召喚	閑却
	取り扱い	宇頂天	蚊柱	該当	韓国	缶切り	残菊
	圧伏	独英	貨幣	憤慨	看護	勘定	喫茶店
c	維持	液滴	可決	概略	感情	紀元	旧式
	意志	各駅	課長	垣間見る	簡素	軌範	同級生
	椅子	悦楽	綿菓子	比較	閑寂	頑張る	供給
d	委託	検閲	寡婦	威嚇的	終刊号	指揮	糾明
	医者	演芸会	禍根	拡大	完璧	珍奇	巨人
	胃袋	拝謁	絶佳	内閣	遺憾な	騎兵	距離
e	以内	王妃	餓鬼	輪郭	司令官	棄権	協会
	小尉	宴会	優雅	核兵器	借款	汽笛	享受
	緯度	救援	祝賀	収穫	博物館	将棋	状況
f	行為	往時	紹介	生活	楽観的	季候	郵便局
	領域	金田翁	楷書	干潟	漢字	規制	凶悪
	威力	応酬	鬼界	括弧	棺おけ	希求	海峡
g	壱万円	欧州	階段	管轄	歓楽	岐路	斤目
	里芋	震央	誘拐	褐色	監視	議論	殺菌
	衆院	億兆	器械	喝采	軍艦	意義	均衡

CHAPTER 2
Weeks 8 – 14

⌒	緊	吟	禁
8 a	キン	ギン	キン

A Tight Recital in Jail.

緊	キン	tight, compact	緊
緊張	きんちょう	tension	8 a
張	チョウ、は-る	stretch	8 a
吟	ギン	recite	吟
吟詠	ぎんえい	recital	8 a
詠	エイ、よ-む	poem, recite, compose	8 a
禁	キン	ban, forbid	禁
禁錮	きんこ	imprisonment; confinement	8 a
錮	コ ふさ.ぐ	to tie	8 a

⌒	銀	句	区
8 b	ギン	ク	ク

A Silver Haiku of Distinction.

銀	ギン	silver	銀
銀河	ぎんが	milky way	8 b
河	カ、かわ	river	8 b
句	ク	phrase, clause	句
俳句	はいく	haiku	8 b
俳	ハイ	amusement, actor	8 b
区	ク	ward, section	区
区別	くべつ	distinction	8 b
別	ベツ、わかれる	split, differ, special	8 b

⌒	偶	具	遇
8 c	グウ	グ	グウ

Fortuitously, the Instruments were found at the Reception.

偶	グウ	by chance, spouse, doll	偶
偶然	ぐうぜん	by chance	8 c
然	ゼン、ネン	duly, thus, so, but	8 c
具	グ	equip, means	具
道具	どうぐ	tool, instrument, implement	8 c
道	ドウ、トウ、みち	way, road	8 c
遇	グウ	meet, receive, treat	遇
待遇	たいぐう	reception	8 c
待	タイ、ま-つ	wait	8 c

⌒	訓	屈	繰
8 d	クン	クツ	くる

Instructions on Cramped Transfers.

訓	クン	instruct, advise	訓
訓言	くんげん	admonitory speech	8 d
言	ゲン、ゴン、いう、こと	word, say, speak	8 d
屈	クツ	submit, crouch	屈
窮屈	きゅうくつ	narrow, cramped	8 d
窮	キュウ、きわめる	distress, extreme	8 d
繰	くる	reel, turn	繰
繰り越す	くりこす	transfer	8 d
越	エツ、こす、こえる	cross, exceed	8 d

⌒	勲	郡	軍
8 e	クン	グン	グン

A Medal for the Rural Sergeant.

勲	クン	merit	勲
勲章	くんしょう	medal	8 e
章	ショウ	badge, chapter	8 e
郡	グン	county, district	郡
郡県	ぐんけん	counties and prefectures	8 e

県	ケン	prefecture	8 e
軍	グン	military, army	軍
軍曹	ぐんそう	sergeant	8 e
曹	ソウ	official, companion	8 e

⌒	系	啓	刑
8 f	ケイ	ケイ	ケイ

A Connection of less than Edifying Criminal Cases.

系	ケイ	lineage, connection	系
系統	けいとう	system, line	8 f
統	トウ、すべる	supervise, lineage	8 f
啓	ケイ	enlighten, state	啓
啓発	けいはつ	enlightenment; edification	8 f
発	ハツ、ホツ	discharge, start, leave	8 f
刑	ケイ	punish	刑
刑事事件	けいじじけん	criminal case	8 f
事	ジ、ズ、こと	thing, matter, act	8 f
件	ケン	affair, case, matter	8 f

⌒	警	径	景
8 g	ケイ	ケイ	ケイ

The Policeman Directly went to the Scene.

警	ケイ	warn, approach	警
警官	けいかん	policeman	8 g
官	カン	government, official	8 g
径	ケイ	path, direct	径
径行	けいこう	going right ahead	8 g
行	コウ、ギョウ、アン、いく	go, conduct, column	8 g
景	ケイ	scene, view, bright	景
景色	けしき	scenery	8 g
色	ショク、シキ、いろ	colour, sensuality	8 g

◇	慶	芸	渓
9 a	ケイ	ゲイ	ケイ

Obscure Comedy in the Valley of darkness.

慶	ケイ	joy	慶
慶弔	けいちょう	congratulations and condolences	9 a
弔	チョウ、とむらう	mourn, funeral	9 a
芸	ゲイ	art, skill, plant	芸
芸人	げいにん	entertainer	9 a
人	ジン、ニン、ひと	person	9 a
渓	ケイ	valley, gorge	渓
渓谷	けいこく	valley, gorge	9 a
谷	コク、たに	valley, gorge	9 a

◇	劇	傑	憲
9 b	ゲキ	ケツ	ケン

A Comedy of Outstanding Officials.

劇	ゲキ	drama, intense	劇
喜劇	きげき	comedy	9 b
喜	キ、よろこぶ	rejoice, happy	9 b
傑	ケツ	outstanding	傑
豪傑	ごうけつ	hero, great man	9 b
豪	ゴウ	strength, splendour, Australia	9 b
憲	ケン	law, constitution	憲
官憲	かんけん	officials; authorities	9 b
官	カン	government, official	9 b

◇	倹	県	検
9 c	ケン	ケン	ケン

The Frugal Prefectural Office dispatched one Inspector.

倹	ケン	thrifty, frugal	倹
倹約	けんやく	frugality	9 c
約	ヤク	promise, summarise, approximately	9 c
県	ケン	prefecture	県
県庁	けんちょう	prefectural office	9 c
庁	チョウ	government, office, agency	9 c
検	ケン	investigate	検
検査員	けんさいん	inspector	9 c
査	サ	investigate	9 c
員	イン	member, official	9 c

◇	件	券	圏
9 d	ケン	ケン	ケン

A Subject concerning New Banknotes and the old Communist Bloc.

件	ケン	affair, matter	件
件名	けんめい	subject; title	9 d
名	メイ、ミョウ、な	name, fame	9 d
券	ケン	ticket, pass, bond	券
新券	しんけん	new banknote	9 d
新	シン、あたらしい、あらた	new	9 d
圏	ケン	range, sphere	圏
共産圏	きょうさんけん	Communist Bloc	9 d
共	キョウ、とも	together	9 d
産	サン、うむ、うまれる、うぶ	birth, produce	9 d

◇	玄	顕	謙
9 e	ゲン	ケン	ケン

The Mysterious Microscope revealed Humble origins.

玄	ゲン	occult, black	玄
幽玄	ゆうげん	mystery	9 e
幽	ユウ	dark, obscure, faint, lonely	9 e

顕	ケン	manifest, visible	顕
顕微鏡	けんびきょう	microscope	9 e
微	ビ	tiny, obscure, secretive	9 e
鏡	キョウ、がかみ	mirror	9 e
謙	ケン	humble, modest	謙
謙遜	けんそん	humble; humility; modesty	9 e
遜	ソン、へりくだる	humble	9 e

◇	弧	孤	個
9 f	コ	コ	コ

A(r)chingly Lonely Individuals.

◇	護	娯	碁
9 g	ゴ	ゴ	ゴ

Lawyers Take Delight in Trays filled with billable clients.

護	ゴ	defend, protect	護
弁護士	べんごし	lawyer	9 g
弁	ベン	speech, know, valve	9 g
士	シ	warrior, scholar, man	9 g
娯	ゴ	pleasure, amusement	娯
娯楽	ごらく	pleasure	9 g
楽	ガク、ラク、たのしい	pleasure, music	9 g
碁	ゴ	go	碁
碁盤	ごばん	checkerboard	9 g
盤	バン	tray, board, bowl, plate	9 g

♣	午	校	郊
10 a	ゴ	コウ	コウ

Boys' Day at a School in the Suburbs.

午	ゴ	noon	午

端午	たんご	Boys' Day (May 5)	10 a
端	タン、はし、は、はた	extremity, edge, bit	10 a
校	コウ	school, (printing) proof	校
高校	こうこう	senior high school	10 a
高	コウ、たかい、たかまる	tall, high, sum	10 a
郊	コウ	suburbs	郊
郊外	こうがい	suburbs	10 a
外	ガイ、ゲ、そと、ほか	outside, other, undo	10 a

⇓	項	鉱	孝
10 b	コウ	コウ	コウ

Is this under the Heading of Coal Pits or Filial Piety?

項	コウ	clause, item, nape	項
項目	こうもく	clause, item	10 b
目	モク、ボク、め、ま	eye, ordinal suffix	10 b
鉱	コウ	mineral, ore	鉱
炭鉱	たんこう	coal mine; coal pit	10 b
炭	タン、すみ	charcoal, coal	10 b
孝	コウ	filial piety	孝
孝行	こうこう	filial piety	10 b
行	コウ、ギョウ、アン、いく	go, conduct, column	10 b

⇓	衡	酵	稿
10 c	コウ	コウ	コウ

An uneasy Balance between Yeast and Straw.

衡	コウ	scales, yoke	衡
均衡	きんこう	balance	10 c
均	キン	level	10 c
酵	コウ	ferment, yeast	酵
発酵	はっこう	fermentation	10 c
発	ハツ、ホツ	discharge, start, leave	10 c

稿	コウ	manuscript, straw	稿
原稿	げんこう	manuscript	10 c
原	ゲン、はら	plain, origin	10 c

⇩	航	康	洪
10 d	コウ	コウ	コウ

On a Voyage to Health and plenty of Water.

航	コウ	sail, voyage	航
航空	こうくう	flight	10 d
空	クウ、そら、あく、あける、から	sky, empty	10 d
康	コウ	peace, health	康
健康	けんこう	health	10 d
健	ケン、すこやか	healthy	10 d
洪	コウ	flood, vast	洪
洪水	こうすい	flood	10 d
水	スイ、みず	water	10 d

⇩	坑	抗	侯
10 e	コウ	コウ	コウ

The Marquis vigorously Resisted a Coal Mine near his property.

侯	コウ	marquis, lord	侯
侯爵	こうしゃく	marquis	10 e
爵	シャク	baron	10 e
抗	コウ	resist, oppose	抗
抵抗	ていこう	resistance	10 e
抵	テイ	resist, match	10 e
坑	コウ	mine, pit, hole	坑
炭坑	たんこう	coal mine	10 e
炭	タン、すみ	charcoal, coal	10 e

⇩	后	拘	講

10 f	コウ	コウ	コウ

Lese-majeste can end in Arrest according to the Lecture.

后	コウ	empress, behind, later	后
太后	たいこう	empress dowager	10 f
太	タイ、タ、ふとい	fat, big	10 f
拘	コウ	seize, adhere to	拘
拘引	こういん	arrest, custody	10 f
引	イン、ひく、ひける	pull, draw	10 f
講	コウ	lecture	講
講義	こうぎ	lecture	10 f
義	ギ	righteousness	10 f

	肯	購	恒
10 g	コウ	コウ	コウ

An Affirmation to Buy Constantly.

肯	コウ	consent, agree, vital	肯
肯定	こうてい	affirmation	10 g
定	テイ、ジョウ、さだめる	fix, establish	10 g
購	コウ	buy	購
購買	こうばい	buying	10 g
買	バイ、かう	buy	10 g
恒	コウ	always, constant	恒
恒常	こうじょう	constancy	10 g
常	ジョウ、つね、とこ	usual, always	10 g

	孔	号	拷
11 a	コウ	ゴウ	ゴウ

The Pupil sent an SOS to save her from Torture.

孔	コウ		hole, Confucius	孔

瞳孔	どうこう	pupil	11 a
瞳	トウ、ドウ、ひとみ	pupil	11 a
号	ゴウ	number, call	号
遭難信号	そうなんしんごう	SOS	11 a
遭	ソウ、あう	encounter, meet	11 a
難	ナン、かたい、むずかしい	difficult, trouble	11 a
信	シン	trust, believe	11 a
拷	ゴウ	torture, hit	拷
拷問	ごうもん	torture	11 a
問	モン、とう、とい、とん	ask	11 a

◇	剛	豪	克
11 b	ゴウ	ゴウ	コク

The Mighty Australian Hero Diligently hit a little ball.

剛	ゴウ	strength	剛
剛健	ごうけん	fortitude	11 b
健	ケン、すこやか	healthy	11 b
豪	ゴウ	strength, Australia	豪
豪傑	ごうけつ	hero, great man	11 b
傑	ケツ	outstanding	11 b
克	コク	conquer, overcome	克
克明	こくめい	diligence	11 b
明	メイ、ミョウ、あかるい	clear, open, bright	11 b

◇	獄	穀	酷
11 c	ゴク	コク	コク

In Prison the Cereals are Harsh.

獄	ゴク	prison, litigation	獄
獄内	ごくない	in prison	11 c
内	ナイ、ダイ、うち	inside	11 c
穀	コク	grain, cereals	穀

穀物	こくもつ	cereals	11 c
物	ブツ、モツ、もの	thing	11 c
酷	コク	severe, cruel, harsh	酷
苛酷	かこく	harsh	11 c
苛	カ、いじめる、さいなむ	torment; scold; chastise	11 c

❖	墾	婚	昆
11 d	コン	コン	コン

That barren patch ought to be Reclaimed for Marrying the Multitudes!

墾	コン	cultivate, reclaim	墾
開墾	かいこん	reclamation	11 d
開	カイ、ひらく、あく	open	11 d
婚	コン	marriage	婚
婚姻	こんいん	marriage	11 d
姻	イン	marriage	11 d
昆	コン	multitude, insect	昆
昆虫	こんちゅう	insect	11 d
虫	チュウ、むし	insect, worm	11 d

❖	佐	紺	詐
11 e	サ	コン	サ

The blushing Assistant lied about a Dark Blue Fraud.

佐	サ	assist, assistant	佐
補佐	ほさ	assistance	11 e
補	ホ、おぎなう	make good, stopgap	11 e
紺	コン	dark blue, dye	紺
紺色	こんいろ	dark blue	11 e
色	ショク、シキ、いろ	colour, sensuality	11 e
詐	サ	lie, deceive	詐
詐欺	さぎ	fraud	11 e
欺	ギ、あざむく	cheat, deceive	11 e

◇	査	才	宰
11 f	サ	サイ	サイ

A keen Investigation into a Thick Prime Minister.

査	サ	investigate	査
調査	ちょうさ	investigation	11 f
調	チョウ、しらべる	adjust, investigate, tune	11 f
才	サイ	talent, year of age	才
鈍才	どんさい	stupidity	11 f
鈍	ドン、にぶい、にぶる	blunt, dull	11 f
宰	サイ	administer	宰
宰相	さいしょう	prime minister	11 f
相	ソウ、ショウ、あい	mutual, minister, aspect	11 f

◇	債	斎	栽
11 g	サイ	サイ	サイ

The Creditor in her Study looks like a Miniature Potted Plant.

債	サイ	debt, loan	債
債権者	さいけんしゃ	creditor	11 g
権	ケン、ゴン	right, authority, balance	11 g
者	シャ、もの	person	11 g
斎	サイ	purification, worship, study	斎
書斎	しょさい	a study	11 g
書	ショ、かく	write	11 g
栽	サイ	planting	栽
盆栽	ぼんさい	bonsai	11 g
盆	ボン	tray, bon festival	11 g

♠	材	崎	剤
12 a	ザイ	さき	ザイ

On Tree-clad Cape Gargantua I reached out for a Painkiller.

材	ザイ	timber, resource	材
材木	ざいもく	wood, lumber	12 a
木	ボク、モク、き、こ	tree, wood	12 a
崎	さき	cape, steep	崎
長崎	ながさき	Nagasaki	12 a
長	チョウ、ながい	long, senior	12 a
剤	ザイ	medicine, drug	剤
鎮痛剤	ちんつうざい	painkiller	12 a
鎮	チン、しずめる、しずまる	calm, suppress	12 a
痛	ツウ、いたい、いたむ	pain, painful	12 a

⛩	昨	索	柵
12 b	サク	サク	サク

Yesterday's Free Thinking becomes today's mental Enclosure.

昨	サク	yesterday, past	昨
昨日	さくじつ	yesterday	12 b
日	ニチ、ジツ、ひ、か	sun, day	12 b
索	サク	rope, search	索
思索	しさく	speculation; meditation	12 b
思	シ、おもう	think	12 b
柵	サク	stockade; fence; wier	柵
鉄柵	てっさく	iron railing	12 b
鉄	テツ	iron, steel	12 b

⛩	錯	策	咲
12 c	サク	サク	さく

Confusing Poor Policies make certain careers Blossom.

錯	サク	mix up, confuse	錯
錯誤	さくご	mistake	12 c
誤	ゴ、あやまる	mistake, mis-	12 c

策	サク	policy, plan, whip	策
拙策	せっさく	poor policy	12 c
拙	セツ	clumsy, poor	12 c
咲	さ-く	blossom	咲
咲き誇る	さきほこる	to be in fullness of bloom	12 c
誇	コ、ほこる	proud, boast	12 c

♠	挨	皿	察
12 d	サツ	さら	サツ

All Hail the Ashtray Police.

挨	サツ	imminent	挨
挨拶	あいさつ	greetings	12 d
挨	アイ	push open	12 d
皿	さら	dish, bowl, plate	皿
灰皿	はいざら	ashtray	12 d
灰	カイ、はい	ashes	12 d
察	サツ	judge, surmise, realise	察
警察	けいさつ	police	12 d
警	ケイ	warn, approach	12 d

♠	算	賛	桟
12 e	サン	サン	サン

He who Reckons knows the number of Praiseworthy Beams in the Jetty.

算	サン	calculate	算
推算	すいさん	calculate, reckon, estimate	12 e
推	スイ、おす	infer, push ahead	12 e
賞	ショウ	prize, praise	賞
賞賛	しょうさん	praise, admire	12 e
賛	サン	praise	12 e
桟	サン	spar, beam, frame	桟

桟橋	さんばし	jetty	12 e
橋	キョウ、はし	bridge	12 e

♠	視	詩	暫
12 f	シ	シ	ザン

Gaze upon beauty and listen to Poetry for a While.

視	シ	see, look, regard	視
可視	かし	visibility	12 f
可	カ	approve, can, should	12 f
詩	シ	poetry	詩
詩抄	ししょう	selected poems	12 f
抄	ショウ	excerpt, extract	12 f
暫	ザン	a while, briefly	暫
暫時	ざんじ	short time	12 f
時	ジ、とき	time	12 f

♠	師	史	資
12 g	シ	シ	シ

Armies, Past and Present, consume huge Capital Resources.

師	シ	teacher, model, army	師
師匠	ししょう	master	12 g
匠	ショウ	craftsman, plan	12 g
史	シ	history, chronicler	史
現代史	げんだいし	contemporary history	12 g
現	ゲン、あらわれる	appear, exist, now	12 g
代	ダイ、タイ、かわる	replace, world, fee	12 g
資	シ	capital, resources	資
資本	しほん	capital	12 g
本	ホン、もと	root, true, book, this	12 g

♠	士	司	詞
13 a	シ	シ	シ

University Graduates and Mcs are prone to ditransitive Verbs.

士	シ	warrior, scholar, man	士
学士	がくし	university graduate	13 a
学	ガク、まなぶ	study	13 a
司	シ	administer, official	司
司会者	しかいしゃ	master of ceremonies	13 a
会	カイ、エ、あう	meet	13 a
者	シャ、もの	person	13 a
詞	シ	word, part of speech	詞
動詞	どうし	verb	13 a
動	ドウ、うごく	move	13 a

♀	嗣	誌	肢
13 b	シ	シ	シ

A Successor to the notorious Journal of Body Limbs.

嗣	シ	heir, succeed to	嗣
嗣子	しし	heir	13 b
子	シ、ス、こ	child	13 b
誌	シ	record, journal	誌
雑誌	ざっし	magazine	13 b
雑	ザツ、ゾウ	miscellany	13 b
肢	シ	limb, part	肢
肢体	したい	the limbs	13 b
体	タイ、テイ、からだ	body	13 b

♀	璽	祉	磁
13 c	ジ	シ	ジ

No Imperial Seal means no Welfare State and no glazed Porcelain.

璽	ジ	imperial seal	璽
御璽	ぎょじ	imperial seal	13 c

御	ギョ、ゴ、おん	drive, honorable	13 c
祉	シ	well-being, happiness	祉
福祉国家	ふくしこっか	welfare state	13 c
福	フク	good fortune	13 c
国	コク、くに	country, region	13 c
家	カ、ケ、いえ、や	house, specialist	13 c
磁	ジ	magnet, porcelain	磁
磁石	じしゃく	magnet	13 c
石	セキ、シャク、いし	stone, rock	13 c

⚲	識	滋	式
13 d	シキ	ジ	シキ

It is Common Sense to provide Nourishment at a Funeral.

識	シキ	knowledge	識
常識	じょうしき	common sense	13 d
常	ジョウ、つね、とこ	usual, always	13 d
滋	ジ	luxuriant, rich, strengthen	滋
滋養	じょう	nourishment	13 d
養	ヨウ、やしなう	rear, support	13 d
式	シキ	ceremony, form	式
葬式	そうしき	funeral	13 d
葬	ソウ、ほうむる	bury	13 d

⚲	疾	軸	芝
13 e	シツ	ジク	しば

Crook Shaft of the Lawnmower.

疾	シツ	illness, swiftly	疾
疾患	しっかん	disease	13 e
患	カン、わずらう	disease, afflicted	13 e
軸	ジク	axle, shaft, scroll	軸
軸物	じくもの	scroll picture	13 e

物	ブツ、モツ、もの	thing	13 e
芝	しば	lawn, turf	芝
芝刈り機	しばかりき	lawnmower	13 e
刈	か-る	reap, cut, shear	13 e
機	キ、はた	loom, device, occasion	13 e
⚱	赦	邪	舎
13 f	シャ	ジャ	シャ

Clemency for Offenders in the Countryside.

赦	シャ	forgiveness	赦
赦免	しゃめん	clemency	13 f
免	メン、まぬかれる	escape, avoid	13 f
邪	ジャ	wickedness	邪
邪悪	じゃあく	wickedness	13 f
悪	アク、オ、わるい	bad, hate	13 f
舎	シャ	house, quarters	舎
田舎	いなか*	countryside	13 f
田	デン、た	rice field	13 f

⚱	爵	尺	釈
13 g	シャク	シャク	シャク

Baron Shakuhachi was asked to Explain himself.

爵	シャク	baron	爵
侯爵	こうしゃく	marquis	13 g
侯	コウ	marquis, lord	13 g
尺	シャク	measure, foot	尺
尺八	しゃくはち	shakuhachi (instr.)	13 g
八	ハチ、や、やっつ、よう	eight	13 g
釈	シャク	explain, release	釈
解釈	かいしゃく	interpretation	13 g
解	カイ、ゲ、とく、とかす	explain, solve	13 g

✏	珠	朱	樹
14 a	シュ	シュ	ジュ

Black Pearls on Vermillion Leather.

珠	シュ	jewel, pearl	珠
真珠	しんじゅ	pearl	14 a
真	シン、ま	true, quintessence	14 a
朱	シュ	vermillion, red	朱
朱肉	しゅにく	red ink pad	14 a
肉	ニク	meat, flesh	14 a
樹	ジュ	tree, stand	樹
樹皮	じゅひ	bark	14 a
皮	ヒ、かわ	skin, leather	14 a

✏	需	儒	週
14 b	ジュ	ジュ	シュウ

Strong Demand for Confucianism in the Weekend.

需	ジュ	need, demand	需
需要	じゅよう	demand	14 b
要	ヨウ、い-る	need, vital, pivot	14 b
儒	ジュ	Confucianism	儒
儒教	じゅきょう	Confucianism	14 b
教	キョウ、おしえる	teach	14 b
週	シュウ	week	週
週末	しゅうまつ	weekend	14 b
末	マツ、バツ、すえ	end, tip	14 b

✏	酬	囚	銃
14 c	シュウ	シュウ	ジュウ

A Reward for Arresting nasty Johnny Gunman.

酬	シュウ	reward, toast, reply	酬
報酬	ほうしゅう	reward	14 c
報	ホウ、むくいる	report, reward	14 c
囚	シュウ	captured, criminal, arrest	囚
虜囚	りょしゅう	captive	14 c
虜	リョ	captive, capture	14 c
銃	ジュウ	gun	銃
拳銃	けんじゅう	pistol	14 c
拳	ケン、こぶし	fist	14 c

♂	粛	叔	淑
14 d	シュク	シュク	シュク

Solemn Uncle took vows of Chastity, poverty, and obedience.

粛	シュク	solemn, quiet	粛
静粛	せいしゅく	silent, still, quiet	14 d
静	セイ、ジョウ、しずか	quiet, calm	14 d
叔	シュク	uncle, young brother	叔
叔父*	おじ	uncle	14 d
父	フ、ちち	father	14 d
淑	シュク	pure, graceful	淑
貞淑	ていしゅく	chastity	14 d
貞	テイ	chastity, virtue	14 d

♂	塾	術	俊
14 e	ジュク	ジュツ	シュン

The magical Juku produced Wizards of Genius.

塾	ジュク	juku (cramschool)	塾
塾長	じゅくちょう	head of juku	14 e
長	チョウ、ながい	long, senior	14 e
術	ジュツ	means, technique	術
仙術	せんじゅつ	wizardry; secret of immortality	14 e

仙	セン	hermit, wizard	14 e
俊	シュン	excellence, genius	俊
俊英	しゅんえい	excellence; genius	14 e
英	エイ	superior, England	14 e

♂	準	准	順
14 f	ジュン	ジュン	ジュン

Prepare to Ratify the Procedure.

準	ジュン	level, conform, quasi-	準
準備	じゅんび	preparation	14 f
備	ビ、そなえる、そなわる	equip, prepare	14 f
准	ジュン	quasi-, conform, permit	准
批准	ひじゅん	ratification	14 f
批	ヒ	criticise, strike, pass	14 f
順	ジュン	sequence, compliance	順
手順	てじゅん	process; procedure	14 f
手	シュ、て、た	hand	14 f

♂	殉	純	旬
14 g	ジュン	ジュン	ジュン

The Martyrdom of a Pure soul in a Ten Day Period.

殉	ジュン	dutiful death	殉
殉教	じゅんきょう	martyrdom	14 g
教	キョウ、おしえる、おそわる	teach	14 g
純	ジュン	pure	純
純朴	じゅんぼく	simplicity, naïve	14 g
朴	ボク	simple, magnolia	14 g
旬	ジュン	ten day period	旬
下旬	げじゅん	last part of month	14 g
下	カ、ゲ、した、しも、もと	base, under, lower	14 g

	8	9	10	11	12	13	14
a	緊張	慶弔	端午	瞳孔	材木	学士	真珠
	吟詠	芸人	高校	遭難信号	長崎	司会者	朱肉
	禁錮	渓谷	郊外	拷問	鎮痛剤	動詞	樹皮
b	銀河	喜劇	項目	剛健	昨日	嗣子	需要
	俳句	豪傑	炭鉱	豪傑	思索	雑誌	儒教
	区別	官憲	孝行	克明	鉄柵	肢体	週末
c	偶然	倹約	均衡	獄内	錯誤	御璽	報酬
	道具	県庁	発酵	穀物	拙策	福祉国家	虜囚
	待遇	検査員	原稿	苛酷	咲き誇る	磁石	拳銃
d	訓言	件名	航空	開墾	挨拶	常識	静粛
	窮屈	新券	健康	婚姻	灰皿	滋養	叔父*
	繰り越す	共産圏	洪水	昆虫	警察	葬式	貞淑
e	勲章	幽玄	侯爵	補佐	推算	疾患	塾長
	郡県	顕微鏡	抵抗	紺色	賞賛	軸物	仙術
	軍曹	謙遜	炭坑	詐欺	桟橋	芝刈り機	俊英
f	系統	弧形	太后	調査	可視	赦免	準備
	啓発	孤立	拘引	鈍才	詩抄	邪悪	批准
	刑事事件	個人	講義	宰相	暫時	田舎	手順
g	警官	弁護士	肯定	債権者	師匠	侯爵	殉教
	径行	娯楽	購買	書斎	現代史	尺八	純朴
	景色	碁盤	恒常	盆栽	資本	解釈	下旬

CHAPTER 3
Weeks 15 – 21

	署	遵	循
15 a	ショ	ジュン	ジュン

An Official always Abides by the Law and Adheres to the rules.

署	ショ	government, office, sign	署
署員	しょいん	official	15 a
員	イン	member, official	15 a
遵	ジュン	follow, obey	遵
遵法	じゅんぽう	law abiding	15 a
法	ホウ、ハッ、ホッ	law	15 a
循	ジュン	follow	循
循守	じゅんしゅ	adherence; compliance	15 a
守	シュ、ス、まもる	protect, keep	15 a

	処	庶	序
15 b	ショ	ショ	ジョ

Management of the Multitude requires a System.

処	ショ	deal with, place	処
処理	しょり	management	15 b
理	リ	reason, principle	15 b
庶	ショ	multitude, various, illegitimate	庶
庶民	しょみん	hoi polloi	15 b
民	ミン、たみ	people, populace	15 b
序	ジョ	beginning, order	序
秩序	ちつじょ	order, system	15 b
秩	チツ	order, stipend	15 b

	叙	晶	徐
15 c	ジョ	ショウ	ジョ

A Description of Liquid Crystal Going Slowly.

叙	ジョ		describe, confer	叙
叙術	じょじゅつ		description	15 c
術	ジュツ		means, technique	15 c
晶	ショウ		crystal, clear, bright	晶
液晶	えきしょう		liquid crystal	15 c
液	エキ		liquid	15 c
徐	ジョ		slowly, gradually	徐
徐行	じょこう		going slowly (car,)	15 c
行	コウ、ギョウ、アン、いく		go, conduct, column	15 c

✎	訟	証	症
15 d	ショウ	ショウ	ショウ

The Plaintiff showed Proof of the Symptoms.

訟	ショウ	accuse, sue	訟
訴訟人	そしょうにん	plaintiff	15 d
訴	ソ、うったえる	sue, appeal	15 d
人	ジン、ニン、ひと	person	15 d
証	ショウ	proof	証
証明	しょうめい	proof	15 d
明	メイ、ミョウ、あかるい	clear, open, bright	15 d
症	ショウ	symptom, illness	症
症状	しょうじょう	symptoms	15 d
状	ジョウ	condition, letter	15 d

✎	抄	匠	渉
15 e	ショウ	ショウ	ショウ

Poetic and Expert Negotiations.

抄	ショウ	excerpt, extract	抄
詩抄	ししょう	selected poems	15 e
詩	シ	poetry	15 e
匠	ショウ	craftsman, plan	匠

師匠	ししょう	master	15 e
師	シ	teacher, model, army	15 e
渉	ショウ	cross over, liaise	渉
交渉	こうしょう	negotiations	15 e
交	コウ、まじわる	mix, exchange	15 e

✎	肖	硝	衝
15 f	ショウ	ショウ	ショウ

The Portrait was greatly changed after the Nitric Acid Accident.

肖	ショウ	be like, be lucky	肖
肖像	しょうぞう	portrait	15 f
像	ゾウ	image	15 f
硝	ショウ	niter, gunpowder	硝
硝酸	しょうさん	nitric acid	15 f
酸	サン、す-い	acid, bitter	15 f
衝	ショウ	collide, clash, road	衝
衝突	しょうとつ	collision	15 f
突	トツ、つ-く	thrust, lunge, protrude	15 f

✎	彰	祥	章
15 g	ショウ	ショウ	ショウ

Commendations were awarded to Scandalous Chartered accountants.

彰	ショウ	manifest	彰
表彰	ひょうしょう	commendation	15 g
表	ヒョウ、おもて	show, surface	15 g
祥	ショウ	good fortune	祥
不祥事	ふしょうじ	bad omen, scandal	15 g
不	フ、ブ	not, un-, dis-	15 g
事	ジ、ズ、こと	thing, matter, act	15 g
章	ショウ	badge, chapter	章
憲章	けんしょう	charter	15 g

憲	ケン			law, constitution	15 g
v		紹	昭		粧
16 a		ショウ	ショウ		ショウ

An Introduction to Showa Make-Up.

紹	ショウ	introduce, inherit	紹
紹介	しょうかい	introduction	16 a
介	カイ	mediate, shell	16 a
昭	ショウ	bright, light	昭
昭和	しょうわ	Showa (period)	16 a
和	ワ、オ、やわらぐ	Japan, peace, soft	16 a
粧	ショウ	adorn, make up	粧
化粧	けしょう	make-up	16 a
化	カ、ケ、ばける、ばかす	change, bewitch	16 a

v		賞	尚	掌
16 b		ショウ	ショウ	ショウ

In Praise of Lofty Palms.

賞	ショウ	prize, praise	賞
賞賛	しょうさん	praise, admire	16 b
賛	サン	praise	16 b
尚	ショウ	further more, esteem	尚
高尚	こうしょう	loftiness	16 b
高	コウ、たかい、たかまる	tall, high, sum	16 b
掌	ショウ	control, palm (hand)	掌
掌中	しょうちゅう	in one's hand	16 b
中	チュウ、なか	middle, inside, China	16 b

v		称	将	奨
16 c		ショウ	ショウ	ショウ

The So-called Commander put a Bounty on her head.

称	ショウ		name, praise	称
自称	じしょう		self-styled	16 c
自	ジ、シ、みずから		self	16 c
将	ショウ		command, about to	将
将帥	しょうすい		commander	16 c
帥	スイ		commander	16 c
奨	ショウ		urge, encourage	奨
奨励金	しょうれいきん		bounty	16 c
励	レイ、はげむ、はげます		encourage, strive	16 c
金	キン、コン、かね、かな		gold, money, metal	16 c

∀	礁	剰	錠
16 d	ショウ	ジョウ	ジョウ

On the Hidden Reef a large Surplus of Handcuffs were found.

礁	ショウ		(hidden) reef	礁
岩礁	がんしょう		reef	16 d
岩	ガン、いわ		rock, crag	16 d
剰	ジョウ		surplus, resides	剰
剰余	じょうよ		surplus	16 d
余	ヨ、あまる、あます		excess, ample, I	16 d
錠	ジョウ		lock, tablet	錠
手錠	てじょう		handcuffs	16 d
手	シュ、て、た		hand	16 d

∀	状	浄	条
16 e	ジョウ	ショウ	ジョウ

In these Circumstances a Clean Act is required.

状	ジョウ		condition, letter	状
状態	じょうたい		condition; situation	16 e
態	タイ		appearance, intent	16 e

浄	ジョウ	pure, clean	浄
浄化	じょうか	purification	16 e
化	カ、ケ、ばける、ばかす	change, bewitch	16 e
条	ジョウ	clause, item, line	条
条例	じょうれい	regulation, law	16 e
例	レイ、たとえる	example, precedent	16 e

v	冗	壌	嬢
16 f	ジョウ	ジョウ	ジョウ

An indelicate Joke about a Down-to-Earth Young Lady.

冗	ジョウ	superfluous	冗
冗談	じょうだん	joke	16 f
談	ダン	conversation, talk	16 f
壌	ジョウ	earth, soil	壌
土壌	どじょう	earth, soil	16 f
土	ド、ト、つち	earth	16 f
嬢	ジョウ	young lady, daughter	嬢
お嬢さん	おじょうさん	young lady, daughter	16 f

v	芯	職	嘱
16 g	シン	ショク	ショク

John Wick's Resignation did not live up to Expectations.

芯	シン	inner part	芯
灯芯	とうしん	wick	16 g
灯	トウ、ひ	light, lamp	16 g
職	ショク	employement, job	職
辞職	じしょく	resignation	16 g
辞	ジ、やめる	word, decline, leave	16 g
嘱	ショク	request, entrust	嘱
嘱望	しょくぼう	expectation	16 g
望	ボウ、モウ、のぞむ	wish, hope, gaze	16 g

VB	審	紳	信
17 a	シン	シン	シン

The Jury is out on the Gentleman's Dignity.

審	シン	judge, investigate	審
陪審	ばいしん	jury	17 a
陪	バイ	attend, accompany	17 a
紳	シン	gentleman, belt	紳
紳士	しんし	gentleman	17 a
士	シ	warrior, scholar, man	17 a
信	シン	trust, believe	信
威信	いしん	dignity	17 a
威	イ	authority, threaten	17 a

VB	帥	迅	睡
17 b	スイ	ジン	スイ

Hit the Command for Fast Sleep.

帥	スイ	commander	帥
将帥	しょうすい	commander	17 b
将	ショウ	command, about to	17 b
迅	ジン	fast, intense	迅
迅速	じんそく	quick, prompt, speedy	17 b
速	ソク、はやい、はやめる	speed, fast	17 b
睡	スイ	sleep	睡
睡眠	すいみん	sleep	17 b
眠	ミン、ねむる、ねむい	sleep, sleepy	17 b

VB	随	枢	髄
17 c	ズイ	スウ	ズイ

Random Notes on Pivotal Essence.

随	ズイ	random, follow	随
随筆	ずいひつ	random notes	17 c
筆	ヒツ、ふで	writing brush	17 c
枢	スウ	pivot, door	枢
中枢	ちゅうすう	centre, pivot	17 c
中	チュウ、なか	middle, inside, China	17 c
髄	ズイ	marrow	髄
真髄	しんずい	essence	17 c
真	シン、ま	true, quintessence	17 c

VB	崇	杉	寸
17 d	スウ	すぎ	スン

Worshipping Rows of Tiny Cedars.

崇	スウ	lofty, noble, revere	崇
崇拝	すうはい	worship	17 d
拝	ハイ、おがむ	worship, respectful	17 d
杉	すぎ	cryptomeria, cedar	杉
杉並木	すぎなみき	avenue of cedars	17 d
並	ヘイ、なみ、ならべる	row, line, ordinary	17 d
木	ボク、モク、き、こ	tree, wood	17 d
寸	スン	measure, inch	寸
一寸	いっすん	tiny bit, one inch	17 d
一	イチ、イツ、ひとつ	one	17 d

VB	是	牲	瀬
17 e	ゼ	セイ	せ

The Proper way to Sacrifice in the Straits.

是	ゼ	proper, this	是
是正	ぜせい	correction	17 e
正	セイ、ショウ、ただしい	correct	17 e
牲	セイ	sacrifice	牲

犠牲	ぎせい		sacrifice	17 e
犠	ギ		sacrifice	17 e
瀬	せ		shallows, rapids	瀬
瀬戸	せと		strait, channel	17 e
戸	コ、と		door	17 e

VB	聖	制	征
17 f	セイ	セイ	セイ

Sagacious System of Subjugation.

聖	セイ	saint, sage, sacred	聖
聖像	せいぞう	sacred image, icon	17 f
像	ゾウ	image	17 f
制	セイ	system, control	制
規制	きせい	regulation, control	17 f
規	キ	standard, measure	17 f
征	セイ	subjugate, travel	征
征服	せいふく	subjugation	17 f
服	フク	clothes, yield, serve	17 f

VB	製	税	斉
17 g	セイ	ゼイ	セイ

Manufacture of Tax-free Togetherness.

製	セイ	manufacture	製
既製	きせい	ready-made	17 g
既	キ、すでに	already, finished	17 g
税	ゼイ	tax, tithe	税
免税	めんぜい	tax-exempt	17 g
免	メン、まぬかれる	escape, avoid	17 g
斉	セイ	equal, similar	斉
一斉	いっせい	all together	17 g
一	イチ、イツ、ひと、ひとつ	one	17 g

	析	席	籍
18 a	セキ	セキ	セキ

Analysing Seats by Nationality.

析	セキ		devide, analyse	析
分析	ぶんせき		analysis	18 a
分	ブン、フン、ブ、わける		divide, understand	18 a
席	セキ		seat, place	席
列席	れっせき		attend, be present	18 a
列	レツ		row, line	18 a
籍	セキ		register	籍
国籍	こくせき		nationality	18 a
国	コク、くに		country, region	18 a

	隻	績	斥
18 b	セキ	セキ	セキ

Boaty McBoatface Achieved a Boycott.

隻	セキ		ship counter	隻
三隻	さんせき		three ships/boats	18 b
三	サン、み、み-つ、みっつ		three	18 b
績	セキ		achievement, spin	績
業績	ぎょうせき		achievement	18 b
業	ギョウ、ゴウ、わざ		profession, deed	18 b
斥	セキ		repel, reject	斥
排斥	はいすい		boycott	18 b
排	ハイ		reject, push, anti-	18 b

	摂	窃	腺
18 c	セツ	セツ	セン

Healthcare prevents the Stealing of Prostate Glands.

摂	セツ	take, act as a proxy	摂
摂生	せっせい	health care	18 c
生	セイ、ショウ、いきる	life, birth, grow	18 c
窃	セツ	steal, stealthy	窃
窃盗	せっとう	theft	18 c
盗	トウ、ぬすむ	steal	18 c
腺	セン	gland	腺
前立腺	ぜんりつせん	prostate gland	18 c
前	ゼン、まえ	before, front	18 c
立	リツ、リュウ、たつ	stand, rise, leave	18 c

♡	仙	旋	線
18 d	セン	セン	セン

The Wizard Rotated Ultraviolet Rays.

仙	セン	hermit, wizard	仙
仙術	せんじゅつ	wizardry	18 d
術	ジュツ	means, technique	18 d
旋	セン	rotate, turn	旋
旋回	せんかい	rotation	18 d
回	カイ、エ、まわる、まわす	turn, rotate	18 d
線	セン	line	線
紫外線	しがいせん	ultraviolet rays	18 d
紫	シ、むらさき	purple, violet	18 d
外	ガイ、ゲ、そと、ほか	outside, other	18 d

♡	践	遷	栓
18 e	セン	セン	セン

A Practical Transition of Fire Hydrants.

践	セン	step, act	践
実践	じっせん	practice, implantation	18 e
実	ジツ、み、みのる	truth, reality	18 e

遷	セン	move, change, shift	遷
遷移	せんい	transition	18 e
移	イ、うつる、うつす	transfer, move	18 e
栓	セン	stopper, plug, tap	栓
消火栓	しょうかせん	fire hydrant	18 e
火	カ、ひ、ほ	fire	18 e
消	ショウ、きえる、けす	extinguish, consume	18 e

ⓦ	繊	宣	膳
18 f	セン	セン	ゼン

Slender Propaganda displayed on a Small Low Table.

繊	セン	fine, slender	繊
繊細	せんさい	fine, delicate	18 f
細	サイ、ほそい、ほそる	slender, fine	18 f
宣	セン	promulgate, state	宣
宣伝	せんでん	propaganda	18 f
伝	デン、つたわる、つたえる	convey, transmit	18 f
膳	ゼン	small low table	膳
配膳	はいぜん	set the table	18 f
配	ハイ、くばる	distribute	18 f

ⓦ	漸	祖	禅
18 g	ゼン	ソ	ゼン

Gradually Great-Grandmother's Meditation gained ground.

漸	ゼン	gradual advance	漸
漸次	ぜんじ	gradually	18 g
次	ジ、シ、つ-ぐ、つぎ	next, follow	18 g
祖	ソ	ancestor	祖
曽祖母	そうそぼ	great-grandmother	18 g
曽	ソ、ソウ、かつて	formerly; once; before	18 g
母	ボ、はは	mother	18 g

禅	ゼン	meditation	禅
座禅	ざぜん	meditation	18 g
座	ザ、すわる	seat, sit, gather	18 g

▽	措	租	塑
19 a	ソ	ソ	ソ

The Next Step is to Lease a Figurine.

措	ソ	place, dispose	措
措置	そち	step, action	19 a
置	チ、おく	put, place	19 a
租	ソ	levy, tithe	租
租借	そしゃく	lease	19 a
借	シャク、かりる	borrow, rent	19 a
塑	ソ	model, figurine	塑
塑像	そぞう	figure, figurine	19 a
像	ゾウ	image	19 a

▽	荘	壮	総
19 b	ソウ	ソウ	ソウ

Villa Stamina attracted the Whole Amount.

荘	ソウ	villa, manor, majestic	荘
荘厳	そうごん	majesty	19 b
厳	ゲン、ゴン、おごそか	severe, strict, solemn	19 b
壮	ソウ	manly, strong, fertile	壮
強壮	きょうそう	robustness	19 b
強	キョウ、ゴウ、つよい	strong	19 b
総	ソウ	whole, total	総
総額	そうがく	total amount	19 b
額	ガク、ひたい	forehead	19 b

	燥	層	僧
19 c	ソウ	ソウ	ソウ

The monastry is a Drying Kiln say the Lower Buddhist Priests.

燥	ソウ	dry, parch	燥
乾燥窯	かんそうがま	drying kiln	19 c
乾	カン、かわく、かわかす	dry	19 c
窯	ヨウ、かま	kiln, oven	19 c
層	ソウ	stratum, layer	層
下層	かそう	lower classes	19 c
下	カ、ゲ、した、しも、さげる	base, under,	19 c
僧	ソウ	priest	僧
僧侶	そうりょ	Buddhist priest	19 c
侶	リョ、とも	follower	19 c

	曹	像	槽
19 d	ソウ	ゾウ	ソウ

The Sergeant's Image was Reflected in the Water Tank.

曹	ソウ	official, companion	曹
軍曹	ぐんそう	sergeant	19 d
軍	グン	military, army	19 d
像	ゾウ	image	像
映像	えいぞう	reflection; image; picture	19 d
映	エイ、うつる、うつす	reflect, shine	19 d
槽	ソウ	tank, tub, vat	槽
水槽	すいそう	water tank	19 d
水	スイ、みず	water	19 d

	則	即	臓
19 e	ソク	ソク	ゾウ

The Principle of Mental Acuity lies in the Entrails.

則	ソク	rule, model, standard	則
原則	げんそく	principle	19 e
原	ゲン、はら	plain, origin	19 e
即	ソク	immediate, namely	即
即妙	そくみょう	ready wit	19 e
妙	ミョウ	exquisite, strange, mystery	19 e
臓	ゾウ	entrails, viscera	臓
内臓	ないぞう	entrails, viscera	19 e
内	ナイ、ダイ、うち	inside	19 e

♟	族	属	俗
19 f	ゾク	ゾク	ゾク

The Family's Affectionate Argot.

族	ゾク	clan, family	族
家族	かぞく	family	19 f
家	カ、ケ、いえ、や	house, specialist	19 f
属	ゾク	belong, genus	属
付属	ふぞく	attached	19 f
付	フ、つける、つく	attach, apply	19 f
俗	ゾク	worldly, vulgar, custom	俗
俗語	ぞくご	slang	19 f
語	ゴ、かたる、かたらう	tell, speak, talk	19 f

♟	卒	賊	汰
19 g	ソツ	ゾク	タ

Soldiers and Pirates desire Dalliances.

卒	ソツ	soldier, end	卒
卒業	そつぎょう	graduation	19 g
業	ギョウ、ゴウ、わざ	profession, deed	19 g
賊	ゾク	rebel, plunder, injure	賊
海賊	かいぞく	pirate	19 g

海	カイ、うみ	sea	19 g
汰	タ	luxury; select	汰
色恋沙汰	いろこいざた	love affair	19 g
色	ショク、シキ、いろ	colour, sensuality	19 g
恋	レン、こう、こい	love, beloved	19 g
沙	サ、すな	sand	19 g

🔲	駄	堕	惰
20 a	ダ	ダ	ダ

A Cheap, Depraved and Lazy Dadaist tale.

駄	ダ	pack-horse, poor quality	駄
駄物	だもの	cheap goods	20 a
物	ブツ、モツ、もの	thing	20 a
堕	ダ	fall(en), degenerate	堕
堕落	だらく	depravity	20 a
落	ラク、おちる、おとす	fall, drop	20 a
惰	ダ	lazy, inert	惰
惰気	だき	indolence	20 a
気	キ、ケ	spirit	20 a

🔲	泰	妥	胎
20 b	タイ	ダ	タイ

A Serene and Peaceful Womb.

泰	タイ	calm, serene, big, Thai	泰
泰然	たいぜん	composure	20 b
然	ゼン、ネン	duly, thus, so, but	20 b
妥	ダ	peaceful, tranquil	妥
妥結	だけつ	agreement	20 b
結	ケツ、むすぶ、ゆう	bind, join, end	20 b
胎	タイ	womb	胎
胎児	たいじ	fetus	20 b

児	ジ、ニ		child	20 b

凹	隊	逮	態
20 c	タイ	タイ	タイ

The Porci Search Party Arrested an Ursa with Attitude.

隊	タイ	corps, unit	隊
捜索隊	そうさくたい	search party	20 c
捜	ソウ、さがす	investigate	20 c
索	サク	rope, search	20 c
逮	タイ	chase, seize	逮
逮捕	たいほ	arrest	20 c
捕	ホ、とらえる、とらわれる	seize, capture	20 c
態	タイ	appearance, intent	態
態度	たいど	attitude	20 c
度	ド、ト、タク、たび	degree, times	20 c

凹	滝	第	題
20 d	たき	ダイ	ダイ

A Cascade of Pass Marks for today's Homework.

滝	たき	cascade, waterfall	滝
清滝	きよたき	clear waterfall	20 d
清	セイ、ショウ、きよよまる	pure, clean	20 d
第	ダイ	grade, order	第
及第点	きゅうだいてん	pass mark	20 d
及	キュウ、およぶ、および	reach, extend, and	20 d
点	テン	point, mark	20 d
題	ダイ	subject, title	題
宿題	しゅくだい	homework	20 d
宿	シュク、やど、やどる	lodge, shelter, house	20 d

	択	拓	濯
20 e	タク	タク	タク

Choose a Rub or a Rinse.

択	タク	choose, select	択
選択	せんたく	choice	20 e
選	セン、えらぶ	elect	20 e
拓	タク	reclaim, clear, rub	拓
開拓	かいたく	reclamation; cultivation	20 e
開	カイ、ひらく、ひらける	open	20 e
濯	タク	wash, rinse	濯
洗濯	せんたく	washing	20 e
洗	セン、あらう	wash, investigate	20 e

	託	卓	宅
20 f	タク	タク	タク

Commit your Table but keep the House.

託	タク	entrust, commit	託
委託	いたく	commission	20 f
委	イ	committee, entrust to	20 f
卓	タク	table, excel, high	卓
食卓	しょくたく	dining table	20 f
食	ショク、ジキ、くらう	food, eat	20 f
宅	タク	house, home	宅
自宅	じたく	one's own house	20 f
自	ジ、シ、みずから	self	20 f

	諾	但	達
20 g	ダク	ただし	タツ

Consenting to Conditions of Delivery.

諾	ダク	consent, agree	諾
承諾	しょうだく	consent	20 g
承	ショウ、うけたまわる	acquiesce, listen to	20 g
但	ただし	but, however	但
但し付き	ただしずき	condition	20 g
付	フ、つける、つく	attach, apply	20 g
達	タツ	attain	達
配達	はいたつ	delivery	20 g
配	ハイ、くばる	distribute	20 g

⏶	棚	単	誕
21 a	たな	タン	タン

A Bookshelf of Pure and Simple Birthday Books.

棚	たな	shelf, trellis	棚
本棚	ほんだな	bookshelf	21 a
本	ホン、もと	root, true, book, this	21 a
単	タン	simple, single, unit	単
簡単	かんたん	simple, brief	21 a
簡	カン	simple, brief	21 a
誕	タン	birth, deceive	誕
誕生日	たんじょうび	birthday	21 a
生	セイ、ショウ、いきる	life, birth, grow	21 a
日	ニチ、ジツ、ひ、か	sun, day	21 a

⏶	談	丹	胆
21 b	ダン	タン	タン

A Strange Story about a Sincere and Courageous Capybara

談	ダン	conversation, talk	談
奇談	きだん	strange story	21 b
奇	キ	strange, odd	21 b
丹	タン	red, sincere	丹

丹誠	たんせい	sincerity, diligence	21 b
誠	セイ、まこと	sincerity	21 b
胆	タン	liver, gall, courage	胆
大胆	だいたん	bravery	21 b
大	ダイ、タイ、おおきい	big	21 b

👍	段	稚	痴
21 c	ダン	チ	チ

Not all Stairs lead to the Nursery of Simpleminds.

段	ダン	step, grade	段
階段	かいだん	stairs	21 c
階	カイ	story, grade, step	21 c
稚	チ	young, immature	稚
幼稚園	ようちえん	kindergarten	21 c
幼	ヨウ、おさない	infancy	21 c
園	エン、その	garden, park	21 c
痴	チ	foolish	痴
白痴	はくち	idiot	21 c
白	ハク、ビャク、しろ、しら	white	21 c

👍	窒	畜	逐
21 d	チツ	チク	チク

Don't Suffocate the Livestock One by One.

窒	チツ	block up, plug	窒
窒死	ちっし	asphyxia	21 d
死	シ、しぬ	death	21 d
畜	チク	livestock	畜
牧畜	ぼくちく	livestock/cattle raising	21 d
牧	ボク、まき	pasture	21 d
逐	チク	chase, pursue	逐
逐一	ちくいち	one by one	21 d

一	イチ、イツ、ひとつ	one	21 d

⛰	嫡	秩	酎
21 e	チャク	チツ	チュウ

Marry a Legitimate Heir, owner of a System of Distilled Spirits production.

嫡	チャク	legitimate heir	嫡
嫡子	ちゃくし	legal heir	21 e
子	シ、ス、こ	child	21 e
秩	チツ	order, stipend	秩
秩序	ちつじょ	order, system	21 e
序	ジョ	beginning, order	21 e
酎	チュウ	sake	酎
焼酎	しょうちゅう	distilled spirits, Shochu	21 e
焼	ショウ、やく、やける	burn, roast	21 e

⛰	駐	衷	忠
21 f	チュウ	チュウ	チュウ

Park your Inner Feelings of Loyalty for a while.

駐	チュウ	stop, stay	駐
駐車	ちゅうしゃ	parking	21 f
車	シャ、くるま	vehicle, chariot	21 f
衷	チュウ	inner feelings	衷
衷心	ちゅうしん	true feelings	21 f
心	シン、こころ	heart, feelings	21 f
忠	チュウ	loyalty, devotion	忠
忠実	ちゅうじつな	loyal	21 f
実	ジツ、み、みのる	(bear) fruit, truth, reality	21 f

⌂	宙	抽	貯
21 g	チュウ	チュウ	チョ

Imagine some Space for Extracting Savings.

宙	チュウ	space, sky	宙
宇宙	うちゅう	space	21 g
宇	ウ	eaves, roof, heaven	21 g
抽	チュウ	pull, draw out	抽
抽出	ちゅうしゅつ	extraction	21 g
出	シュツ、スイ、でる、だす	emerge, put out	21 g
貯	チョ	store, save	貯
貯蓄	ちょちく	savings	21 g
蓄	チク、たくわえる	accumulate, store	21 g

	15	16	17	18	19	20	21
a	署員	紹介	陪審	分析	措置	駄物	本棚
	遵法	昭和	紳士	列席	租借	堕落	簡単
	循守	化粧	威信	国籍	塑像	惰気	誕生日
b	処理	賞賛	将帥	三隻	荘厳	泰然	奇談
	庶民	高尚	迅速	業績	強壮	妥結	丹誠
	秩序	掌中	睡眠	排斥	総額	胎児	大胆
c	叙術	自称	随筆	摂生	乾燥窯	捜索隊	階段
	液晶	将帥	中枢	窃盗	下層	逮捕	幼稚園
	徐行	奨励金	真髄	前立腺	僧侶	態度	白痴
d	訴訟人	岩礁	崇拝	仙術	軍曹	清滝	室死
	証明	剰余	杉並木	旋回	映像	及第点	牧畜
	症状	手錠	一寸	紫外線	水槽	宿題	逐一
e	詩抄	状態	是正	実践	原則	選択	嫡子
	師匠	浄化	犠牲	遷移	即妙	開拓	秩序
	交渉	条例	瀬戸	消火栓	内臓	洗濯	焼酎
f	肖像	冗談	聖像	繊細	家族	委託	駐車
	硝酸	土壌	規制	宣伝	付属	食卓	衷心
	衝突	お嬢さん	征服	配膳	俗語	自宅	忠実
g	表彰	灯芯	既製	漸次	卒業	承諾	宇宙
	不祥事	辞職	免税	曽祖母	海賊	但し付き	抽出
	憲章	嘱望	一斉	座禅	色恋沙汰	配達	貯蓄

CHAPTER 4
Weeks 22 – 28

🏆	庁	帳	腸
22 a	チョウ	チョウ	チョウ

The Authorities Cancelled Enteritis and other inflamations.

庁	チョウ	government, office	庁
官庁	かんちょう	authorities	22 a
官	カン	government, official	22 a
帳	チョウ	register, drape	帳
帳消し	ちょうけし	cancellation	22 a
消	ショウ、きえる、けす	extinguish, consume	22 a
腸	チョウ	intestine(s)	腸
腸炎	ちょうえん	enteritis	22 a
炎	エン、ほのお	inflammation, flame	22 a

🏆	勅	賃	朕
22 b	チョウ	チン	チン

The Imperial Edict states that Rent is due to the Royal We Musical Review.

勅	チョク	imperial edict	勅
勅語	ちょくご	imperial edict	22 b
語	ゴ、かたる	tell, speak, talk	22 b
賃	チン	wages, fee	賃
家賃	やちん	rent	22 b
家	カ、ケ、いえ、や	house, specialist	22 b
朕	チン	Royal We	朕
朕歌劇団	ちんかげきだん	RW Musical Review	22 b
歌	カ、うた、うたう	song	22 b
劇	ゲキ	drama, intense	22 b
団	ダン、トン	group, body, ball	22 b

🏆	塚	陳	墜
22 c	つか	チン	ツイ

In Takarazuka the Opera Troupe Petitioned against Falling ticket prices.

塚	つか	mound, tumulus	塚
宝塚	たからづ	Takarazuka (PN)	22 c
宝	ホウ、たから	treasure	22 c
陳	チン	state, show, old	陳
陳情	ちんじょう	petition	22 c
情	ジョウ、セイ、なさけ	feeling, pity, fact	22 c
墜	ツイ	fall	墜
墜落	ついらく	fall	22 c
落	ラク、おちる、おとす	fall, drop	22 c

🏆	偵	坪	訂
22 d	テイ	つぼ	テイ

Detection of Floorspace Alteration.

偵	テイ	spy, investigate	偵
探偵	たんてい	detection	22 d
探	タン、さぐる、さがす	search, probe	22 d
坪	つぼ	tsubo, measure	坪
建坪	たてつぼ	floor space	22 d
建	ケン、コン、たてる、たつ	build, erect	22 d
訂	テイ	correct, revise	訂
改訂	かいてい	revision	22 d
改	カイ、あらためる	reform	22 d

🏆	邸	貞	抵
22 e	テイ	テイ	テイ

A Mansion built for Virtuous Resistance.

邸	テイ		mansion, residence	邸
邸宅	ていたく		mansion	22 e
宅	タク		house, home	22 e
貞	テイ		chastity, virtue	貞
貞操	ていそう		chastity	22 e
操	ソウ、みさお、あやつる		handle, chastity	22 e
抵	テイ		resist, match	抵
抵抗	ていこう		resistance	22 e
抗	コウ		resist, oppose	22 e

🏆	逓	艇	廷
22 f	テイ	テイ	テイ

Next Time use a Lifeboat when appearing in a Court of Law.

逓	テイ		relay, in sequence	逓
逓次	ていじ		in order, successively	22 f
次	ジ、シ、つぐ、つぎ		next, follow	22 f
艇	テイ		boat	艇
救命艇	きゅうめいてい		lifeboat	22 f
救	キュウ、すくう		rescue, redeem	22 f
命	メイ、ミョウ、いのち		life, order	22 f
廷	テイ		court, government office	廷
法廷	ほうてい		court of law	22 f
法	ホウ、ハッ、ホッ		law	22 f

🏆	呈	亭	停
22 g	テイ	テイ	テイ

Presenting a Restaurant that is famous for its Power Cuts.

呈	テイ	present, offer	呈
進呈	しんてい	presentation	22 g
進	シン、すすむ、すすめる	advance	22 g
亭	テイ	pavilion, inn	亭
料亭	りょうてい	restaurant	22 g
料	リョウ	materials, charge	22 g
停	テイ	stop	停
停電	ていでん	power cut	22 g
電	デン	electricity	22 g

♀	帝	鉄	適
23 a	テイ	テツ	テキ

An Empire with a Cast Iron Disposition.

帝	テイ	emperor	帝
帝国	ていこく	empire	23 a
国	コク、くに	country, region	23 a
鉄	テツ	iron, steel	鉄
鋳鉄	ちゅうてつ	cast iron	23 a
鋳	チュウ、いる	cast, found, mint	23 a
適	テキ	suitable, fit, go	適
適性	てきせい	aptitude	23 a
性	セイ、ショウ	nature, sex	23 a

♀	迭	哲	徹
23 b	テツ	テツ	テツ

Whirling Philosophers keep it up All Night.

迭	テツ	alternate, rotate	迭
更迭	こうてつ	reshuffle	23 b
更	コウ、さら、ふける	change, again, grow	23 b
哲	テツ	wisdom	哲
哲学	てつがく	philosophy	23 b

学	ガク、まなぶ	study	23 b
徹	テツ	go through, clear, remove	徹
徹夜	てつや	all night	23 b
夜	ヤ、よ、よる	night	23 b

♀ 23 c	撤 テツ	点 テン	典 テン

Removing Blemishes improves the Dictionary.

撤	テツ	remove, withdraw	撤
撤収	てっしゅう	removal	23 c
収	シュウ、おさめる	obtain, store, supply	23 c
点	テン	point, mark	点
斑点	はんてん	speck; fleck	23 c
斑	ハン、まだら	spot; blemish; speck	23 c
典	テン	code, rule, precedent	典
辞典	じてん	dictionary	23 c
辞	ジ、やめる	word, decline, leave	23 c

♀ 23 d	斗 ト	電 デン	展 テン

Big Dipper's Electrifying Display.

斗	ト	dipper, measure	斗
北斗星	ほくとせい	Big Dipper	23 d
星	セイ、ショウ、ほし	star	23 d
北	ホク、きた	north	23 d
電	デン	electricity	電
電灯	でんとう	electric light	23 d
灯	トウ、ひ	light, lamp	23 d
展	テン	unfold	展
展示	てんじ	display	23 d
示	ジ、シ、しめす	show	23 d

	徒	途	奴
23 e	ト	ト	ド

Walking the Road to Future Slavery.

徒	ト、あだ	follower, futility	徒
徒歩	とほ	walking	23 e
歩	ホ、ブ、フ、あるく	walk	23 e
途	ト	road, way	途
前途	ぜんと	future	23 e
前	ゼン、まえ	before, front	23 e
奴	ド	slave, servant	奴
奴隷制	どれいせい	slavery	23 e
隷	レイ	slave, prisoner	23 e
制	セイ	system, control	23 e

	塔	到	塔
23 f	トウ	トウ	トウ

Step on the arrow of time to Arrive at the Tombstone of destination.

搭	トウ	load, board	搭
搭乗	とうじょう	boarding	23 f
乗	ジョウ、のる、のせる	ride, mount, load	23 f
到	トウ	go, reach, arrive	到
到達	とうたつ	arrival	23 f
達	タツ	attain	23 f
塔	トウ	tower, monument	塔
石塔	せきとう	tombstone	23 f
石	セキ、シャク、コク、いし	stone, rock	23 f

	騰	謄	痘
23 g	トウ	トウ	トウ

A Sharp Rise in certified Smallpox Copies.

騰	トウ	rise, leap	騰
暴騰	ぼうとう	sharp rise	23 g
暴	ボウ、バク、あばく	violence, expose	23 g
謄	トウ	copy	謄
謄本	とうほん	manuscript	23 g
本	ホン、もと	root, true, book, this	23 g
痘	トウ	smallpox	痘
天然痘	てんねんとう	smallpox	23 g
天	テン、あめ、あま	heaven, sky	23 g
然	ゼン、ネン	duly, thus, so, but	23 g

☐	糖	陶	党
24 a	トウ	トウ	トウ

The Saccharine Potters Party.

糖	トウ	sugar	糖
砂糖	さとう	sugar	24 a
砂	サ、シャ、すな	sand, gravel, grain	24 a
陶	トウ	ceramic, pottery	陶
陶器	とうき	ceramic ware	24 a
器	キ、うつわ	vessel, utensil, skill	24 a
党	トウ	party, faction	党
政党	せいとう	political party	24 a
政	セイ、ショウ、まつりごと	government	24 a

☐	堂	銅	胴
24 b	ドウ	ドウ	ドウ

And the Dining Hall features a Bronze Statue of Mr. Creosote's Torso.

堂	ドウ	hall, temple	堂
食堂	しょくどう	dining hall	24 b
食	ショク、ジキ、くう、くらう	food, eat	24 b
銅	ドウ	copper	銅

銅像	どうぞう		bronze statue	24 b
像	ゾウ		image	24 b
胴	ドウ		body, trunk, torso	胴
胴体	どうたい		body, trunk	24 b
体	タイ、テイ、からだ		body	24 b

☺	峠	特	篤
24 c	とうげ	トク	トク

A Mountain Pass, in Particular, is no place for having an Episode.

峠	とうげ	mountain pass	峠
峠道	とうげみち	road through a mtn pass	24 c
道	ドウ、トウ、みち	way, road	24 c
特	トク	special	特
特許	とっきょ	patent	24 c
許	キョ、ゆるす	permit, allow, home	24 c
篤	トク	sincere, serious	篤
危篤	きとく	seriously ill	24 c
危	キ、あぶない	dangerous	24 c

☺	徳	匿	督
24 d	トク	トク	トク

Morality's Pseudonym is named Supervision.

徳	トク	virtue	徳
道徳	どうとく	morality	24 d
道	ドウ、トウ、みち	way, road	24 d
匿	トク	conceal	匿
匿名	とくめい	pseudonym	24 d
名	メイ、ミョウ、な	name, fame	24 d
督	トク	supervise, urge	督
監督	かんとく	supervision	24 d
監	カン	supervise, watch	24 d

😀	毒	凸	屯
24 e	ドク	トツ	トン

Addicted to Bulging Barracks.

毒	ドク	poison	毒
中毒	ちゅうどく	poisoning; addiction	24 e
中	チュウ、なか	middle, inside, China	24 e
凸	トツ	convex, protrusion	凸
凸円	とつえん	convexity	24 e
円	エン、まるい	round, yen	24 e
屯	トン	barracks, camp, post	屯
屯営	とんえい	barracks	24 e
営	エイ、いとなむ	conduct, barracks	24 e

😀	弐	匂	那
24 f	ニ	におう	ナ

Twenty Smelly Husbands.

弐	ニ	two	弐
弐拾	にじゅう	twenty	24 f
拾	シュウ、ジュウ、ひろう	pick up, gather, ten	24 f
匂	におう	fragrant; stink; glow	匂
匂い袋	においぶくろ	sachet	24 f
袋	タイ、ふくろ	bag, pouch	24 f
那	ナ	what?	那
旦那	だんな	husband	24 f
旦	タン、ダン	daybreak; dawn	24 f

😀	尿	肉	妊
24 g	ニョウ	ニク	ニン

Urinals and Delicatessen are Pregnant with meaning.

尿	ニョウ	urine	尿
尿意	にょうい	nature's call	24 g
意	イ	mind, thought, will	24 g
肉	ニク	meat, flesh	肉
豚肉	ぶたにく	pork	24 g
豚	トン、ぶた	pig, pork	24 g
妊	ニン	pregnant woman	妊
妊娠	にんしん	pregnancy	24 g
娠	シン	pregnancy	24 g

⊡	念	農	寧
25 a	ネン	ノウ	ネイ

The Will to Farming is more Peaceful than the will to power.

念	ネン	thought, concern	念
念力	ねんりき	will	25 a
力	リョク、リキ、ちから	strength, effort	25 a
農	ノウ	farming	農
農村	のうそん	rural community	25 a
村	ソン、むら	village	25 a
寧	ネイ	peace, preferably	寧
丁寧	ていねい	civility, care	25 a
丁	チョウ、テイ	block, exact	25 a

⊡	脳	能	把
25 b	ノウ	ノウ	ハ

Brain Efficiency is within your Grasp!

脳	ノウ	brain	脳
頭脳	ずのう	brain	25 b
頭	トウ、ズ、ト、あたま	head, counter for animals	25 b
能	ノウ	ability, can, Noh	能
能率	のうりつ	efficiency	25 b

率	ソツ、リツ、ひきいる	rate, command	25 b
把	ハ	grasp, comprehend	把
把握	はあく	grasp	25 b
握	アク、にぎる	grasp, grip	25 b

▫	覇	婆	派
25 c	ハ	バ	ハ

The Ambitious Older Person Dispatched some hellish creatures.

覇	ハ	domination, rule	覇
覇気	はき	ambition	25 c
気	キ、ケ	spirit	25 c
婆	バ	old woman	婆
鬼婆	おにばば	witch, hag	25 c
鬼	キ、おに	devil, demon, ghost	25 c
派	ハ	faction, send	派
派遣	はけん	dispatch	25 c
遣	ケン、つかう、つかわす	send, use, do	25 c

▫	俳	肺	排
25 d	ハイ	ハイ	ハイ

Haiku Lungs received a standing Ovulation.

俳	ハイ	amusement, actor	俳
俳句	はいく	haiku	25 d
句	ク	phrase, clause	25 d
肺	ハイ	lung(s)	肺
肺臓	はいぞう	lungs	25 d
臓	ゾウ	entrails, viscera	25 d
排	ハイ	reject, expel, push, anti-	排
排卵	はいらん	ovulation	25 d
卵	ラン、たまご	egg, ovum, spawn	25 d

・	倍	輩	賠
25 e	バイ	ハイ	バイ

Doubling Seniors require no Compensation.

倍	バイ	double, -fold	倍
倍加	ばいか	doubling	25 e
加	カ、くわえる、くわわる	add, join	25 e
輩	ハイ	fellow, companion	輩
先輩	せんぱい	one's senior	25 e
先	セン、さき	previous, precede, tip	25 e
賠	バイ	compensate	賠
賠償	ばいしょう	compensation	25 e
償	ショウ、つぐなう	recompense, redeem	25 e

・	陪	媒	伯
25 f	バイ	バイ	ハク

The Jury approved of Mediation between the Count and the discounted.

陪	バイ	attend, accompany	陪
陪審	ばいしん	jury	25 f
審	シン	judge, investigate	25 f
媒	バイ	intermediary	媒
媒介	ばいかい	mediation	25 f
介	カイ	mediate, shell	25 f
伯	ハク	count, senior figure	伯
伯父	おじ*	uncle	25 f
父	フ、ちち	father	25 f

・	爆	舶	漠
25 g	バク	ハク	バク

Exploding Ships of the Desert.

爆	バク	burst, explode	爆
爆発	ばくはつ	explosion	25 g
発	ハツ、ホツ	discharge, start, leave	25 g
舶	ハク	ship, shipping	舶
船舶	せんぱく	shipping	25 g
船	セン、ふね、ふな	boat, ship	25 g
漠	バク	vague, vast, desert	漠
砂漠	さばく	desert	25 g
砂	サ、シャ、すな	sand, gravel, grain	25 g

☒	伐	肌	箱
26 a	バツ	はだ	はこ

Punishment for Bare Skin must involve the botox Box.

伐	バツ	attack, cut down	伐
征伐	せいばつ	punishment	26 a
征	セイ	subjugate, travel	26 a
肌	はだ	skin, texture, grain	肌
素肌	すはだ	bare skin	26 a
素	ソ、ス	element, base, bare	26 a
箱	はこ	box	箱
箱入り	はこいり	boxed	26 a
入	ニュウ、いる	to go in, to come in	26 a

☒	繁	閥	班
26 b	ハン	バツ	ハン

Profuse Conglomerates of Rescue Teams.

繁	ハン	profuse, rich, complex	繁
繁雑	はんざつ	complex; intricate	26 b
雑	ザツ、ゾウ	miscellany	26 b
閥	バツ	faction, clan, lineage	閥
財閥	ざいばつ	zaibatsu (conglomerates)	26 b

財	ザイ、サイ	wealth, assets	26 b
班	ハン	squad, group, allot	班
救護班	きゅうごはん	relief squad	26 b
救	キュウ、すくう	rescue, redeem	26 b
護	ゴ	defend, protect	26 b

☒	藩	畔	販
26 c	ハン	ハン	ハン

Feudal Lords near the Lakeside are Selling trinkets.

藩	ハン	fief, clan, fence	藩
藩主	はんしゅ	feudal lord	26 c
主	シュ、ス、ぬし、おも	master, owner, main	26 c
畔	ハン	ridge, edge	畔
湖畔	こはん	lakeside	26 c
湖	コ、みずうみ	lake	26 c
販	ハン	sell, trade	販
販売	はんばい	selling	26 c
売	バイ、うる、うれる	sell	26 c

☒	版	頒	範
26 d	ハン	ハン	ハン

The Publisher Distributed Model cars.

版	ハン	print, board	版
出版者	しゅっぱんしゃ	publisher	26 d
出	シュツ、スイ、でる、だす	emerge, put out	26 d
者	シャ、もの	person	26 d
頒	ハン	distribute, divide	頒
頒布	はんぷ	distribution	26 d
布	フ、ぬの	cloth, spread	26 d
範	ハン	model, norm	範
軌範	きはん	model, example	26 d
軌	キ	track, rut, way	26 d

⊠	搬	般	番
26 e	ハン	ハン	バン

A Conveyor Belt of General Turn coats.

搬	ハン	carry, transport	搬
搬送帯	はんそうたい	conveyor belt	26 e
送	ソウ、おく-る	send	26 e
帯	タイ、お-びる、おび	wear, zone	26 e
般	ハン	general, time, carry	般
一般	いっぱん	general	26 e
一	イチ、イツ、ひとつ	one	26 e
番	バン	turn, number, guard	番
順番	じゅんばん	turn	26 e
順	ジュン	sequence, compliance	26 e

⊠	晩	蛮	盤
26 f	バン	バン	バン

In the Evening Barbarians like to Plate up.

晩	バン	evening, late	晩
今晩	こんばん	this evening	26 f
今	コン、キン、いま	now	26 f
蛮	バン	barbarian	蛮
蛮人	ばんじん	barbarian	26 f
人	ジン、ニン、ひと	person	26 f
盤	バン	tray, board, bowl, plate	盤
水盤	すいばん	bowl	26 f
水	スイ、みず	water	26 f

⊠	非	妃	披
26 g	ヒ	ヒ	ヒ

A Peccadillo was committed at the Royal Reception.

非	ヒ	not, un-, fault	非
非行	ひこう	misdemeanor	26 g
行	コウ、ギョウ、いく	go, conduct, column	26 g
妃	ヒ	queen, princess	妃
王妃	おうひ	queen, princess	26 g
王	オウ	king	26 g
披	ヒ	open, disclose	披
披露宴	ひろうえん	(wedding) reception	26 g
露	ロ、ロウ、つゆ	dew, reveal, Russia	26 g
宴	エン	banquet	26 g

ロ	批	碑	罷
27 a	ヒ	ヒ	ヒ

A Critical Monument to Redundancy.

批	ヒ	criticise, strike	批
批判	ひはん	criticism	27 a
判	ハン、バン	seal; judgement	27 a
碑	ヒ	tombstone	碑
石碑	せきひ	tombstone	27 a
石	セキ、シャク、コク、いし	stone, rock	27 a
罷	ヒ	cease, leave, go	罷
罷免	ひめん	dismissal	27 a
免	メン、まぬかれる	escape, avoid	27 a

ロ	百	微	姫
27 b	ヒャク	ビ	ひめ

Doing 800 Laps for the Smile of a Princess.

百	ヒャク	hundred	百
六百周	ろっぴゃくしゅう	800 laps	27 b
六	ロク、む、むつ	six	27 b
周	シュウ、まわ-り	circumference, around	27 b

微	ビ		tiny, obscure, secretive	微
微笑	びしょう		smile	27 b
笑	ショウ、わらう、えむ		laugh, smile	27 b
姫	ひめ		princess, lady, pretty	姫
姫宮	ひめみや		princess	27 b
宮	キュウ、グウ、みや		palace, shrine, prince	27 b

♀	票	標	評
27 c	ヒョウ	ヒョウ	ヒョウ

Voting confirms the Standard Reputation.

票	ヒョウ	vote, label, sign	票
投票	とうひょう	voting	27 c
投	トウ、な-げる	throw, cast	27 c
標	ヒョウ	sign(post), mark	標
標準	ひょうじゅん	standard	27 c
準	ジュン	level, conform, quasi-	27 c
評	ヒョウ	criticism, comment	評
評判	ひょうばん	reputation	27 c
判	ハン、バン	seal; stamp; judgement	27 c

♀	賓	秒	頻
27 d	ヒン	ビョウ	ヒン

The Guest of Honor enjoyed a Moment of Frequent frissons.

賓	ヒン	guest, visitor	賓
賓客	ひんきゃく	guest of honor	27 d
客	キャク、カク	guest, visitor	27 d
秒	ビョウ	second (of time)	秒
寸秒	すんびょう	a moment	27 d
寸	スン	measure, inch	27 d
頻	ヒン	frequent, frown	頻
頻繁	ひんぱん	frequent, incessant	27 d

| 繁 | ハン | | profuse, rich, complex | 27 d |

🔲	婦	瓶	敏
27 e	フ	ビン	ビン

After the Lady swooned, a Bottle of smelling salt was Quickly produced.

婦	フ	woman, wife	婦
婦人	ふじん	woman; lady; adult female	27 e
人	ジン、ニン、ひと	person	27 e
瓶	ビン	bottle, jug, jar	瓶
花瓶	かびん	flower vase	27 e
花	カ、はな	flower, blossom	27 e
敏	ビン	agile, quick, alert	敏
過敏	かびん	nervousness; oversensitivity	27 e
過	カ、すぎる、すごす	pass, exceed, error	27 e

🔲	府	附	符
27 f	フ	フ	フ

Government Affiliated factions sold Tickets for "kickbacks".

府	フ	government centre	府
政府筋	せいふすじ	government sources	27 f
政	セイ、まつりごと	government	27 f
筋	キン、すじ	muscle, sinew	27 f
附	フ	attach	附
附属	ふぞく	affiliated	27 f
属	ゾク	belong, genus	27 f
符	フ	tally, sign	符
切符	きっぷ	ticket	27 f
切	セツ、サイ、きる	cut	27 f

	扶	賦	普
27 g	フ	フ	フ

Support Monthly Payments for Ordinary corporate raiders.

扶	フ	help, support	扶
扶助	ふじょ	aid	27 g
助	ジョ、たすける、すけ	assist, help	27 g
賦	フ	levy, tribute, ode	賦
月賦	げっぷ	monthly payment	27 g
月	ゲツ、ガツ、つき	moon	27 g
普	フ	widely, generally	普
普通	ふつう	ordinary	27 g
通	ツウ、ツ、とおる	pass, way, commute	27 g

	部	譜	服
28 a	ブ	フ	フク

Only Part of a Musical Score and some Clothing was left.

部	ブ	part, section, clan	部
部分	ぶぶん	part	28 a
分	ブン、フン、ブ、わける	divide, minute	28 a
譜	フ	notation, genealogy	譜
楽譜	がくふ	musical score	28 a
楽	ガク、ラク、たのしい	pleasure, music	28 a
服	フク	clothes, yield, serve	服
被服	ひふく	clothing	28 a
被	ヒ、こうむる	sustain, cover, wear	28 a

	福	副	復
28 b	フク	フク	フク

For that Lavish Side-Job we will go Round the world.

福	フク	good fortune	福
裕福	ゆうふく	opulence	28 b
裕	ユウ	rich, plentyful	28 b
副	フク	deputy, vice-, sub-	副
副業	ふくぎょう	side-job	28 b
業	ギョウ、ゴウ、わざ	profession, deed, karma	28 b
復	フク	again, repeat	復
往復	おうふく	round trip	28 b
往	オウ	go, gone, past	28 b

♀	雰	丙	墳
28 c	フン	ヘイ	フン

An Atmospheric Third-rate Tumulus.

雰	フン	atmosphere, air	雰
雰囲気	ふんいき	atmosphere	28 c
囲	イ、かこむ、かこう	surround	28 c
気	キ、ケ	spirit	28 c
丙	ヘイ	c, 3rd	丙
丙種	へいしゅ	class C; third class	28 c
種	シュ、たね	seed, kind	28 c
墳	フン	(burial-) mound	墳
古墳	こふん	tumulus	28 c
古	コ、ふるい、ふるす	old	28 c

♀	弊	陛	幣
28 d	ヘイ	ヘイ	ヘイ

Evil servants of the Throne were offering precious Coins.

弊	ヘイ	my (humble), evil	弊
弊害	へいがい	evil, abuse	28 d
害	ガイ	harm, damage	28 d
陛	ヘイ	majesty, throne	陛

陛下	へいか		majesty	28 d
下	カ、ゲ、した、しも、さげる		base, under, lower	28 d
幣	ヘイ		offering, money	幣
貨幣	かへい		coin, money	28 d
貨	カ		goods, money	28 d

🔲	塀	遍	弁
28 e	ヘイ	ヘン	ベン

The Earthen Wall of Ubiqitous Compensation.

塀	ヘイ	fence, wall	塀
土塀	どべい	earthen wall	28 e
土	ド、ト、つち	earth	28 e
遍	ヘン	widely, everywhere	遍
普遍性	ふへんせい	universality	28 e
普	フ	widely, generally	28 e
性	セイ、ショウ	nature, sex	28 e
弁	ベン	speech, know, valve	弁
弁償	べんしょう	compensation	28 e
償	ショウ、つぐなう	recompense, redeem	28 e

🔲	勉	簿	舗
28 f	ベン	ボ	ホ

Study Records at the Premises.

勉	ベン	strive	勉
勉強	べんきょう	study	28 f
強	キョウ、ゴウ、つよい	strong	28 f
簿	ボ	register, record(s)	簿
名簿	めいぼ	(name) register	28 f
名	メイ、ミョウ、な	name, fame	28 f
舗	ホ	shop, lay, pave	舗
店舗	てんぽ	shop, store	28 f

店	テン、みせ	store, premises	28 f

早	邦	砲	胞
28 g	ホウ	ホウ	ホウ

Commonwealth of the Cannon and the Womb.

邦	ホウ	country, japan	邦
連邦	れんぽう	commonwealth; federation	28 g
連	レン、つらなる、	accompany, row	28 g
砲	ホウ	gun, cannon	砲
大砲	たいほう	gun, cannon	28 g
大	ダイ、タイ、お-きい	big	28 g
胞	ホウ	placenta, womb	胞
胞子	ほうし	spore	28 g
子	シ、ス、こ	child	28 g

	22	23	24	25	26	27	28
a	官庁	帝国	砂糖	念力	征伐	批判	部分
	帳消し	鋳鉄	陶器	農村	素肌	石碑	楽譜
	腸炎	適性	政党	丁寧	箱入り	罷免	被服
b	勅語	更迭	食堂	頭脳	繁雑	六百周	裕福
	家賃	哲学	銅像	能率	財閥	微笑	副業
	朕歌劇団	徹夜	胴体	把握	救護班	姫宮	往復
c	宝塚	撤収	峠道	覇気	藩主	投票	雰囲気
	陳情	斑点	特許	鬼婆	湖畔	標準	丙種
	墜落	辞典	危篤	派遣	販売	評判	古墳
d	探偵	北斗星	道徳	俳句	出版者	賓客	弊害
	建坪	電灯	匿名	肺臓	頒布	寸秒	陛下
	改訂	展示	監督	排卵	軌範	頻繁	貨幣
e	邸宅	徒歩	中毒	倍加	搬送帯	婦人	土塀
	貞操	前途	凸円	先輩	一般	花瓶	普遍性
	抵抗	奴隷制	屯営	賠償	順番	過敏	弁償
f	逓次	搭乗	弐拾	陪審	今晩	政府筋	勉強
	救命艇	到達	匂い袋	媒介	蛮人	附属	名簿
	法廷	石塔	旦那	伯父	水盤	切符	店舗
g	進呈	暴騰	尿意	爆発	非行	扶助	連邦
	料亭	謄本	豚肉	船舶	王妃	月賦	大砲
	停電	天然痘	妊娠	砂漠	披露宴	普通	胞子

CHAPTER 5
Weeks 29 – 35

	剖	肪	俸
29 a	ボウ	ボウ	ホウ

Anatomy of a Fat Salary.

剖	ボウ	divide, cut up	剖
解剖学	かいぼうがく	anatomy	29 a
解	カイ、ゲ、とく	unravel, explain, solve	29 a
学	ガク、まなぶ	study	29 a
肪	ボウ	fat	肪
脂肪	しぼう	fat	29 a
脂	シ、あぶら	fat, grease, resin	29 a
俸	ホウ	salary, pay	俸
年俸	ねんぽう	annual, salary	29 a
年	ネン、とし	year	29 a

	貿	棒	某
29 b	ボウ	ボウ	ボウ

Trading Truncheons at a Certain Place.

貿	ボウ	trade, exchange	貿
貿易	ぼうえき	trade	29 b
易	エキ、イ、やさしい	easy, divination	29 b
棒	ボウ	pole, bar, club	棒
棒紅	ぼうべに	lipstick	29 b
紅	コウ、ク、べに、くれない	red, crimson, rouge	29 b
某	ボウ	a certain-, some-	某
某所	ぼうしょ	a certain place	29 b
所	ショ、ところ	place, situation	29 b

	僕	朴	帽
29 c	ボク	ボク	ボウ

Public Servants desire Basic Headgear.

僕	ボク	manservant, I	僕
公僕	こうぼく	public servant	29 c
公	コウ、おおやけ	public, fair, lord	29 c
朴	ボク	simple, magnolia	朴
純朴	じゅんぼく	simplicity, naïve, unsophisticated	29 c
純	ジュン	pure	29 c
帽	ボウ	cap, headgear	帽
帽子	ぼうし	hat	29 c
子	シ、ス、こ	child	29 c

🖌	撲	没	堀
29 d	ボク	ボツ	ほり

No Pounding of Collapsing Canals.

撲	ボク	strike, beat	撲
打撲	だぼく	strike, blow	29 d
打	ダ、うつ	hit, strike	29 d
没	ボツ	sink, disappear, die, lack, not	没
陥没	かんぼつ	cave-in, subsidence	29 d
陥	カン、おちいる	collapse	29 d
堀	ほり	moat, ditch, canal	堀
堀川	ほりかわ	canal	29 d
川	セン、かわ	river	29 d

🖌	盆	摩	奔
29 e	ボン	マ	ホン

Miniature Japanese Trees don't like Rubbing and Running.

盆	ボン	tray, bon festival	盆
盆栽	ぼんさい	bonsai	29 e
栽	サイ	planting	29 e
摩	マ	rub, graze, scrape	摩
摩擦	まさつ	friction	29 e

擦	サツ、す-る、すれる	rub, chafe, brush	29 e
奔	ホン	run	奔
奔走	ほんそう	running about, efforts	29 e
走	ソウ、はしる	run	29 e

🔖	毎	枚	魔
29 f	マイ	マイ	マ

Defeating Daily Duplicitous Devils.

毎	マイ	each, every	毎
毎日	まいにち	every day	29 f
日	ニチ、ジツ、ひ、か	sun, day	29 f
枚	マイ	sheet, counter	枚
二枚舌	にまいじた	duplicity	29 f
二	ニ、ふた、ふたつ	two	29 f
舌	ゼツ、した	tongue	29 f
魔	マ	demon, devil	魔
悪魔	あくま	devil (mara)	29 f
悪	アク、オ、わるい	bad, hate	29 f

🔖	又	膜	抹
29 g	また	マク	マツ

Subcontracting Membranes will be Eliminated.

又	また	or again	又
又請け	またうけ	subcontract	29 g
請	セイ、シン、こう、うける	request, undertake	29 g
膜	マク	membrane	膜
網膜	もうまく	retina	29 g
網	モウ、あみ	net, network	29 g
抹	マツ	erase, rub, paint	抹
抹殺	まっさつ	erasure	29 g
殺	サツ、サイ、セツ、ころす	kill	29 g

ㄐ	未	慢	漫
30 a	ミ	マン	マン

Unknown and Offensive Manga Characters.

未	ミ	immature, not yet	未
未詳	みしょう	unknown; unidentified	30 a
詳	ショウ、くわしい	detailed	30 a
慢	マン	lazy, rude, boastful	慢
侮慢	ぶまん	contempt; insult; offence	30 a
侮	ブ、あなどる	scorn, despise	30 a
漫	マン	random, diffuse, involuntary	漫
漫画	まんが	manga	30 a
画	ガ、カク	picture, stroke	30 a

ㄐ	魅	蜜	岬
30 b	ミ	ミツ	みさき

Charming Circe Served Black Treacle on Cape Carmilla.

魅	ミ	bewitch, charm	魅
魅了	みりょう	charm, captivate, hold spellbound	30 b
了	リョウ	complete, finish, understand	30 b
蜜	ミツ	honey; nectar; molasses	蜜
蜂蜜	はちみつ	honey	30 b
蜂	ホウ、はち	bee; wasp; hornet	30 b
岬	みさき	promontory, cape	岬

ㄐ	妙	密	脈
30 c	ミョウ	ミツ	ミャク

Mysteriously Dense Mountain Ranges.

妙	ミョウ	exquisite, strange, mystery	妙
玄妙	げんみょう	mystery	30 c

玄	ゲン	occult, black	30 c
密	ミツ	dense, secret	密
密度	みつど	density	30 c
度	ド、ト、タク、たび	degree, times	30 c
脈	ミャク	vein, pulse	脈
山脈	さんみゃく	mountain range	30 c
山	サン、やま	mountain	30 c

凵	娘	盟	銘
30 d	むすめ	メイ	メイ

The Son-in-law rose to the top of the Federation of Brand Names.

娘	むすめ	daughter, girl	娘
娘婿	むすめむこ	son-in-law	30 d
婿	セイ、むこ	son-in-law	30 d
盟	メイ	alliance, pledge	盟
連盟	れんめい	federation	30 d
連	レン、つらなる、つれる	accompany, row	30 d
銘	メイ	inscribe, sign	銘
銘柄	めいがら	brand	30 d
柄	ヘイ、がら、え	handle, pattern, power	30 d

凵	紋	盲	猛
30 e	モン	モウ	モウ

Conventional Blind Fury was unleashed.

紋	モン	(family) crest, pattern	紋
紋切れ型	もんきれがた	conventional	30 e
切	セツ、サイ、きる	cut	30 e
型	ケイ、かた	type, model, mould	30 e
盲	モウ	blind	盲
文盲	もんもう	illiteracy	30 e
文	ブン、モン、ふみ	writing, text	30 e

猛	モウ	fierce, raging, brave	猛
猛烈	もうれつな	fierce	30 e
烈	レツ	fierce, intense	30

ㄐ	約	輸	厄
30 f	ヤク	ユ	ヤク

No Booking required to Export Bad Fortune.

約	ヤク	promise, summarise	約
予約	よやく	booking	30 f
予	ヨ	already, prior, I	30 f
輸	ユ	transport, send	輸
輸出	ゆしゅつ	export	30 f
出	シュツ、スイ、でる	emerge, put out	30 f
厄	ヤク	misfortune, disaster	厄
災厄	さいやく	calamity	30 f
災	サイ、わざわい	calamity	30 f

ㄐ	悠	裕	愉
30 g	ユウ	ユウ	ユ

Proceed Calmly to Opulence and Pleasure.

悠	ユウ	compose, distant, long time	悠
悠然	ゆうぜん	calmly	30 g
然	ゼン、ネン	duly, thus, so, but	30 g
裕	ユウ	rich, plentyful	裕
裕福	ゆうふく	opulence	30 g
福	フク	good fortune	30 g
愉	ユ	joy, pleasure	愉
愉快	ゆかい	pleasure	30 g
快	カイ、こころよい	pleasant, cheerful	30 g

モ	幽	郵	猶

31 a	ユウ	ユウ	ユ

At that Spectral Post Office delivery has been Deferred for a long time.

幽	ユウ	dark, obscure, faint	幽
幽霊	ゆうれい	ghost	31 a
霊	レイ、リョウ、たま	spirit, soul	31 a
郵	ユウ	mail, relay station	郵
郵便局	ゆうびんきょく	post office	31 a
便	ベン、ビン、たより	convenience, mail	31 a
局	キョク	office, section, end	31 a
猶	ユウ	moreover, still, hesitate	猶
猶予	ゆうよ	postponement; deferment	31 a
予	ヨ	already, prior	31 a

31 b	予	融	陽
	ヨ	ユウ	ヨウ

Our Anticipation of Financial gains dissolved like snow in the Sun.

予	ヨ	already, prior,	予
予期	よき	expectation; anticipation	31 b
期	キ、ゴ	period, expect	31 b
融	ユウ	dissolve, melt	融
金融	きんゆう	finance	31 b
金	キン、コン、かね	gold, money, metal	31 b
陽	ヨウ	sunny, male, positive	陽
太陽	たいよう	sun	31 b
太	タイ、タ、ふとい	fat, big	31 b

31 c	曜	容	洋
	ヨウ	ヨウ	ヨウ

Consider reading every Day of the Week a Relaxing Western Book.

曜	ヨウ	day of the week	曜
曜日	ようび	day of the week	31 c
日	ニチ、ジツ、ひ、か	sun, day	31 c
容	ヨウ	contain, looks	容
寛容	かんよう	tolerance	31 c
寛	カン	magnanimous, relax	31 c
洋	ヨウ	ocean, western	洋
洋書	ようしょ	Western book	31 c
書	ショ、かく	write	31 c

モ	翌	擁	庸
31 d	ヨウ	ヨウ	ヨウ

Next Time, let's Embrace a Banal activity.

翌	ヨク	next (of time)	翌
翌日	よくじつ	next day	31 d
日	ニチ、ジツ、ひ、か	sun, day	31 d
擁	ヨウ	embrace, protect	擁
抱擁	ほうよう	embrace	31 d
抱	ホウ、だく、いだく	embrace, hug, hold	31 d
庸	ヨウ	ordinary, work	庸
凡庸	ぼんよう	banality	31 d
凡	ボン、ハン	mediocre, common, roughly	31 d

モ	羅	欄	酪
31 e	ラ	ラン	ラク

Comprehensive Columns of Cheese.

羅	ラ	gauze, net, include	羅
網羅的	もうらてき	comprehensive	31 e
網	モウ、あみ	net, network	31 e
的	テキ、まと	target, -like, adj. suffix	31 e
欄	ラン	column, railing, space	欄

欄干	らんかん	railing	31 e
干	カン、ほす、ひる	dry, defense	31 e
酪	ラク	curd, dairy produce	酪
乾酪	かんらく	cheese	31 e
乾	カン、かわく	dry	31 e

毛	理	覧	濫
31 f	リ	ラン	ラン

It's Unreasonable and offensive to go Sightseeing in a Flooded area.

理	リ	reason, rational	理
無理	むり	unreasonable	31 f
無	ム、ブ、ない	not, non, cease to be	31 f
覧	ラン	see, look	覧
巡覧	じゅんらん	tour, sightseeing	31 f
巡	ジュン、めぐる	go around	31 f
濫	ラン	flood, overdo, wanton	濫
氾濫	はんらん	overflowing; flood	31 f
氾	ハン、ひろがる	spread out; wide	31 f

毛	璃	吏	痢
31 g	リ	リ	リ

In the Bunraku Play, the Official with Diarrhea was a big hit.

璃	リ	glassy	璃
操浄瑠璃	あやつりじょうるり	name for bunraku	31 g
浄	ジョウ	pure, clean	31 g
瑠	ル	lapis lazuli	31 g
操	ソウ、みさお、あやつる	handle, chastity	31 g
吏	リ	official	吏
公吏	こうり	public official	31 g
公	コウ、おおやけ	public, fair, lord	31 g
痢	リ	diarrhea	痢

下痢	げり		diarrhea	31 g
下	カ、ゲ、した、しも		base, under	31 g

▓	略	隆	陸
32 a	リャク	リュウ	リク

Outlines of a Prosperous Landmass.

略	リャク	abbreviate, outline	略
概略	がいりゃく	outline	32 a
概	ガイ	roughly, in general	32 a
隆	リュウ	high, peak, prosper	隆
隆盛	りゅうせい	prosperity	32 a
盛	セイ、ジョウ、もる	prosper, serve	32 a
陸	リク	land	陸
陸塊	りくかい	landmass	32 a
塊	カイ、かたまり	lump, clod, mass	32 a

▓	虜	慮	硫
32 b	リョ	リョ	リュウ

A Captured Reserve of Sulfuric Acid.

虜	リョ	captive, capture	虜
虜囚	りょしゅう	captive	32 b
囚	シュウ	captured, criminal, arrest	32 b
慮	リョ	thought, concern	慮
遠慮	えんりょ	reserve	32 b
遠	エン、オン、とおい	distant	32 b
硫	リュウ	sulfur	硫
硫酸	りゅうさん	sulfuric acid	32 b
酸	サン、すい	acid, bitter	32 b

▓	了	猟	料
32 c	リョウ	リョウ	リョウ

After Completing the Hunt, the game is delivered to the Restaurant.

了	リョウ	complete, finish, understand	了
完了	かんりょう	completion, conclusion	32 c
完	カン	complete	32 c
猟	リョウ	game-hunting	猟
狩猟	しゅりょう	hunting	32 c
狩	シュ、かる、かり	hunt	32 c
料	リョウ	materials, measure, charge	料
料亭	りょうてい	restaurant	32 c
亭	テイ	pavilion, inn	32 c

▓	僚	両	領
32 d	リョウ	リョウ	リョウ

One Colleague controlled one bank and the Boss Possessed the other.

僚	リョウ	colleague, official	僚
同僚	どうりょう	colleague	32 d
同	ドウ、おなじ	same	32 d
両	リョウ	both, pair, coin	両
両岸	りょうがん	both banks (of a river)	32 d
岸	ガン、きし	bank, shore	32 d
領	リョウ	control, possess, chief, territory	領
領袖	りょうしゅう	leader; chief; boss	32 d
袖	シュウ、そで	sleeve; wing ; extension	32 d

▓	厘	寮	療
32 e	リン	リョウ	リョウ

Only Tiny numbers of Boarding Students can be Cured.

厘	リン	rin, tiny amount	厘
厘毛	りんもう	a trifle	32 e
毛	モウ、け	hair	32 e

寮	リョウ		hostel, dormitory	寮
寮生	りょうせい		boarding student	32 e
生	セイ、ショウ、いきる		life, birth, grow	32 e
療	リョウ		cure, heal	療
療法	りょうほう		remedy	32 e
法	ホウ、ハッ、ホッ		law	32 e

	塁	瑠	倫
32 f	ルイ	ル	リン

Basically this Lapis Lazuli is Unequalled.

塁	ルイ	fort, baseball, base	塁
塁審	るいしん	base umpire	32 f
審	シン	judge, investigate	32 f
瑠	ル	lapis lazuli	瑠
瑠璃色	るりいろ	lapis lazuli blue; azure	32 f
璃	リ	glassy	32 f
色	ショク、シキ、いろ	colour, sensuality	32 f
倫	リン	principles, ethics	倫
絶倫	ぜつりん の	matchless; unequalled	32 f
絶	ゼツ、たえる、たやす	cease, sever, end	32 f

	令	零	累
32 g	レイ	レイ	ルイ

The Commander Froze the Sum Total.

令	レイ	order, rule	令
司令官	しれいかん	commander	32 g
司	シ	administer, official	32 g
官	カン	government, official	32 g
零	レイ	zero, tiny, fall	零
零下	れいか	below zero	32 g
下	カ、ゲ、した、しも	base, under, lower	32 g

累	ルイ	accumulate, involve	累
累計	るいけい	sum total	32 g
計	ケイ、はかる	measure	32 g

🔊 33 a	歴 レキ	隷 レイ	齢 レイ

The History of Slavery goes back many Years.

歴	レキ	history	歴
歴史	れきし	history	33 a
史	シ	history, chronicler	33 a
隷	レイ	slave, prisoner	隷
奴隷制	どれいせい	slavery	33 a
奴	ド	slave, servant, guy	33 a
制	セイ	system, control	33 a
齢	レイ	age	齢
年齢	ねんれい	age, years	33 a
年	ネン、とし	year	33 a

🔊 33 b	錬 レン	列 レツ	烈 レツ

Training a Line-up of Heroines.

錬	レン	refine, train, drill	錬
鍛錬	たんれん	forge, train	33 b
鍛	タン、きたえる	forge, train	33 b
列	レツ	row, line	列
列席	れっせき	attend, be present	33 b
席	セキ	seat, place	33 b
烈	レツ	fierce, intense	烈
烈女	れつじょ	heroine	33 b
女	ジョ、ニョ、おんな、め	woman	33 b

	楼	廉	炉
33 c	ロウ	レン	ロ

And the Bell Tower comes with a Bargain Blast Furnace.

楼	ロウ	tower	楼
鐘楼	しょうろう	bell tower	33 c
鐘	ショウ、かね	bell	33 c
廉	レン	honest, cheap, angle	廉
廉価	れんか	low price	33 c
価	カ、あたい	price, value, worth	33 c
炉	ロ	furnace	炉
高炉	こうろ	blast furnace	33 c
高	コウ、たか-い、たか	tall, high, sum	33 c

	労	浪	廊
33 d	ロウ	ロウ	ロウ

A Tired Drifter floated into the Picture Gallery.

労	ロウ	labor, toil	労
疲労	ひろう	fatigue	33 d
疲	ヒ、つかれる、つからす	tire, exhaustion	33 d
浪	ロウ	wave, drift, waste	浪
浪人	ろうにん	drifter	33 d
人	ジン、ニン、ひと	person	33 d
廊	ロウ	walkway	廊
画廊	がろう	picture gallery	33 d
画	ガ、カク	picture, stroke	33 d

	郎	録	論
33 e	ロウ	ロク	ロン

Taro's Record is up for Discussion.

郎	ロウ		man, husband	郎
太郎	たろう		Taro (name)	33 e
太	タイ、タ、ふとい、ふとる		fat, big	33 e
録	ロク		record, inscribe	録
記録	きろく		record	33 e
記	キ、しるす		account, chronicle	33 e
論	ロン		argument, opinion	論
討論	とうろん		debate, discussion	33 e
討	トウ、うつ		attack	33 e

▭	湾	♎	枠
33 f	ワン	♎	わく

The safe Harbour is definitely Within Limits.

湾	ワン	bay, gulf	湾
港湾	こうわん	harbour	33 f
港	コウ、みなと	harbour	33 f
枠	わく	frame	枠
枠内	わくない	within limits	33 f
内	ナイ、ダイ、うち	inside	33 f

Part 2
Kanji with Multiple Readings

	曖	哀	握
33 g	♎	♉	♎

Ambiguous and Pitiful Grasp.

曖	アイ、かげる	dark; not clear	曖
曖昧	あいまい	vague; ambiguous	33 g
昧	マイ、くらい	dark; foolish	33 g
哀	アイ、あわれ、あわれむ	sorrow, pity	哀
悲哀	ひあい	sadness	33 g
悲	ヒ、かなしい、かなしむ	sad	33 g
握	アク、にぎる	grasp, grip	握
把握	はあく	grasp	33 g
把	ハ	grasp, comprehend	33 g

✝	安	宛	暗
34 a	♎	♉	♎

Safe Address on the Dark Side.

安	アン、やすい	restful, ease, cheap	安
安全	あんぜん	safety	34 a
全	ゼン、まったく	whole, completely	34 a
宛	エン、あて、ずつ	address	宛
宛先	あてさき	address	34 a
先	セン、さき	previous, precede, tip	34 a
暗	アン、くらい	dark, gloomy	暗
暗黒面	あんこくめん	dark or seamy side	34 a
黒	コク、くろ、くろい	black	34 a
面	メン、おも、おもて	face, aspect, mask	34 a

✝	位	闇	衣
34 b	♎	♉	♎

An Academic Twilight Undresser.

位	イ、くらい	rank, extent	位
学位	がくい	academic degree	34 b
学	ガク、まなぶ	study	34 b
闇	アン、くらい、やみ	get dark; gloom; disorder	闇
夕闇	ゆうやみ	dusk; twilight	34 b
夕	セキ、ゆう	evening	34 b
衣	イ、ころも	garment	衣
脱衣	だつい	undressing	34 b
脱	ダツ、ぬぐ、ぬげる	take off, shed, escape	34 b

十	畏	偉	慰
34 c	♎	♉	♎

Fearful Heroes crave for Solace.

畏	イ, おそ.れる、かしこまる	fear, graciously	畏
畏怖	いふ	awe; fear; fright	34 c
怖	フ、こわい	fear, afraid	34 c
偉	イ、えらい	great, grand	偉
偉人	いじん	hero, prodigy	34 c
人	ジン、ニン、ひと	person	34 c
慰	イ、なぐさめる、なぐさむ	confort, console	慰
慰安	いあん	solace, relaxation	34 c
安	アン、やすい	restful, ease, cheap	34 c

十	違	異	菱
34 d	♎	♉	♎

Different stages of Alien Atrophy.

違	イ、ちがう、ちがえる	differ	違
相違	そうい	difference	34 d
相	ソウ、ショウ、あい	mutual, minister	34 d
異	イ、こと	differ, strange	異
異人	いじん	alien, foreigner	34 d

人	ジン、ニン、ひと	person	34 d
萎	イ、な、しおれる	wither; droop; lame	萎
萎縮	いしゅく	atrophy	34 d
縮	シュク、ちぢむ、ちぢまる	shrink, reduce	34 d

╋	依	育	彙
34 e	♎	♉	♎

Depending on Enriching Vocabulary.

依	イ、エ	depend, as is	依
依存症	いぞんしょう	(drug) dependence	34 e
存	ソン、ゾン	exist, know, think	34 e
症	ショウ	symptom, illness	34 e
育	イク、そだつ	raise, educate	育
肥育	ひいく	fattening	34 e
肥	ヒ、こえる、こえ	fatten, enrich	34 e
彙	イ、はりねずみ	classify; hedgehog	彙
語彙	ごい	vocabulary; lexicon	34 e
語	ゴ、かたる、かたらう	tell, speak, talk	34 e

╋	逸	印	茨
34 f	♎	♉	♎

Excellent Impressons of the Thorn Hedge.

逸	イツ	escape, go astray, fast	逸
秀逸	しゅういつ	excellence	34 f
秀	シュウ、ひいでる	excel, excellent	34 f
印	イン、しるし	seal, sign, symbol	印
印象	いんしょう	impression	34 f
象	ショウ、ゾウ	elephant, image	34 f
茨	シ、いばら	briar; thorn	茨
茨垣	いばらがき	thorn hedge	34 f
垣	かき	fence, hedge	34 f

✢	淫	因	咽
34 g	♎	♉	♎

Lust Causes the Throat to be Choked.

淫	イン、ひたす、ほしいまま	licentiousness	淫
淫欲	いんよく	lust	34 g
欲	ヨク、ほっする、ほしい	greed, desire	34 g
因	イン、よる	cause, be based on	因
因果	いんが	cause-and-effect	34 g
果	カ、はたす、はてる	fruit, result	34 g
咽	イン、エン、エツ、むせぶ	throat; choked	咽
咽喉	いんこう	throat	34 g
喉	コウ、のど	throat; voice	34 g

✢	陰	隠	飲
35 a	♎	♉	♎

The Plot's Cover-up was hard to Swallow.

陰	イン、かげ、かげる	shadow, negative	陰
陰謀	いんぼう	plot, intrigue	35 a
謀	ボウ、ム、はかる	plot, stratagem	35 a
隠	イン、かくす、かくれる	hide	隠
隠蔽	いんぺい	concealment; cover-up	35 a
蔽	ヘイ、おおう	cover; shade; mantle	35 a
飲	イン、のむ	drink, swallow	飲
飲助	のみすけ	drunkard	35 a
助	ジョ、たすける	assist, help	35 a

✢	雨	右	羽
35 b	♎	♉	♎

Raindrops keep falling on the Right Wing.

雨	ウ、あめ、あま	rain	雨
雨垂れ	あまだれ	raindrops	35 b
垂	スイ、たれる、たらす	suspend, hang down	35 b
右	ウ、ユウ、みぎ	right	右
右派	うは	rightist faction	35 b
派	ハ	faction, send	35 b
羽	ウ、は、はね	wing, bird counter	羽
羽毛	うもう	plumage	35 b
毛	モウ、け	hair	35 b

✣	運	影	雲
35 c	♎	♉	♎

Moving Shot of Drifting Clouds.

運	ウン、はこぶ	transport, luck, move	運
運動	うんどう	movement	35 c
動	ドウ、うごく、うごかす	move	35 c
影	エイ、かげ	shadow, light, image	影
撮影	さつえい	photography	35 c
撮	サツ、とる	pluck, take	35 c
雲	ウン、くも	cloud	雲
浮雲	うきぐも	drifting cloud	35 c
浮	フ、うく、うかれる	float, fleeting, gay	35 c

✣	泳	栄	永
35 d	♎	♉	♎

When winning the Swimming Race, wear Laurels for Eternity.

泳	エイ、およぐ	swim	泳
競泳	きょうえい	swimming race	35 d
競	キョウ、ケイ、きそう、せる	compete, vie for	35 d
栄	エイ、さかえる、はえる	flourish	栄

栄冠	えいかん		laurels	35 d
冠	カン、かんむり		crown	35 d
永	エイ、ながい		long, lasting	永
永遠	えいえん		eternity	35 d
遠	エン、オン、とおい		distant	35 d

✠	鋭	液	疫
35 e	♎	♉	♎

Spirited Blood Types hold out against an Epidemic.

鋭	エイ、するどい		sharp, keen	鋭
気鋭	きえい		spirited, energetic	35 e
気	キ、ケ		spirit	35 e
液	エキ		liquid	液
血液型	けつえきがた		blood type	35 e
血	ケツ、ち		blood	35 e
型	ケイ、かた		type, model, mould	35 e
疫	エキ、ヤク		epidemic	疫
疫病	えきびょう		epidemic	35 e
病	ビョウ、ヘイ、やまい		illness	35 e

✠	鋭	液	疫
35 f	♎	♉	♎

No Regrets, even with Profits Delayed.

怨	エン、オン、ウン、うらむ		grudge; resentment	怨
怨恨	えんこん		grudge	35 f
恨	コン、うらむ、うらめしい		resent, regret	35 f
益	エキ、やく		gain, profit, benefit	益
利益	りえき		profit	35 f
利	リ、きく		profit, gain, effect	35 f
延	エン、のびる、のべる		extend, postpone	延
延着	えんちゃく		delayed arrival	35 f

着	チャク、ジャク、きる	arrive, wear	35 f

✠	沿	猿	煙
35 g	♎	♉	♎

Near the Coast line an Ape Man disappeared in a Cloud of Dust.

沿	エン、そう	go, alongside	沿
沿岸	えんがん	coast	35 g
岸	ガン、きし	bank, shore	35 g
猿	エン、さる	monkey, ape	猿
猿人	えんじん	ape man	35 g
人	ジン、ニン、ひと	person	35 g
煙	エン、けむる、けむり、けむい	smoke	煙
土煙	つちけむり	cloud of dust	35 g
土	ド、ト、つち	earth	35 g

	29	30	31	32	33	34	35
a	解剖学	未詳	幽霊	概略	歴史	安全	陰謀
	脂肪	侮慢	郵便局	隆盛	奴隷制	宛先	隠蔽
	年俸	漫画	猶予	陸塊	年齢	暗黒面	飲助
b	貿易	魅了	予期	虜囚	鍛錬	学位	雨垂れ
	棒紅	蜂蜜	金融	遠慮	列席	夕闇	右派
	某所	岬	太陽	硫酸	烈女	脱衣	羽毛
c	公僕	玄妙	曜日	完了	鐘楼	畏怖	運動
	純朴	密度	寛容	狩猟	廉価	偉人	撮影
	帽子	山脈	洋書	料亭	高炉	慰安	浮雲
d	打撲	娘婿	翌日	同僚	疲労	相違	競泳
	陥没	連盟	抱擁	両岸	浪人	異人	栄冠
	堀川	銘柄	凡庸	領袖	画廊	萎縮	永遠
e	盆栽	紋切れ型	網羅的	厘毛	太郎	依存症	気鋭
	摩擦	文盲	欄干	寮生	記録	肥育	血液型
	奔走	猛烈	乾酪	療法	討論	語彙	疫病
f	毎日	予約	無理	呈審	港湾	秀逸	怨恨
	二枚舌	輸出	巡覧	瑠璃色	枠内	印象	利益
	悪魔	災厄	氾濫	絶倫	33 f	茨垣	延着
g	又請け	悠然	操浄瑠璃	司令官	曖昧	淫欲	沿岸
	網膜	裕福	公吏	零下	悲哀	因果	猿人
	抹殺	愉快	下痢	累計	把握	咽喉	土煙

CHAPTER 6
Weeks 36 – 42

‡	縁	鉛	艶
36 a	♎	♉	♎

An Ominous tale of the Pencil and the Voluptuous one.

縁	エン、ふち	relation(s), ties, fate	縁
縁起	えんぎ	omen	36 a
起	キ、おきる、おこる	arise, cause	36 a
鉛	エン、なまり	lead	鉛
鉛筆	えんぴつ	pencil	36 a
筆	ヒツ、ふで	writing brush	36 a
艶	エン、あでやか、つや	glossy; luster; charm	艶
妖艶	ようえん	voluptuous	36 a
妖	ヨウ、あやしい、なまめく	attractive	36 a

‡	汚	塩	凹
36 b	♎	♉	♎

All staff in the Laundry room have Salty, Cavernous Eyes.

汚	オ、けがす、よごす	dirt, dishonour	汚
汚れ物	よごれもの	laundry	36 b
物	ブツ、モツ、もの	thing	36 b
塩	エン、しお	salt	塩
塩水	しおみず	salt water	36 b
水	スイ、みず	water	36 b
凹	オウ、くぼむ、へこむ	hollow, concave, dent	凹
凹眼	おうがん	cavernous eyes	36 b
眼	ガン、ゲン、まなこ	eye	36 b

‡	旺	押	奥
36 c	♎	♉	♎

A Fit model pushed the Barrow Deep into the beauty parlor.

旺	オウ	flourishing; beautiful	旺
旺盛	おうせい	full of vim and vigor	36 c
盛	セイ、ジョウ、もる	prosper, heap, serve	36 c
押	オウ、おす	push	押
手押し車	ておしぐるま	barrow	36 c
手	シュ、て、た	hand	36 c
奥	オウ、おく	heart, interior	奥
奥底	おくそこ	depths	36 c
底	テイ、そこ	bottom, base	36 c

⚥	横	黄	岡
36 d	♎	♉	♎

Show your Profile on the Yellow Knoll.

横	オウ、よこ	side, cross ways	横
横顔	よこがお	profile	36 d
顔	ガン、かお	face	36 d
黄	コウ、オウ、き、こ	yellow	黄
黄色	きいろ	yellow	36 d
色	ショク、シキ、いろ	color, sensuality	36 d
岡	コウ、おか	hill; height; knoll	岡
静岡	しずおか	Shizuoka (city)	36 d
静	セイ、ジョウ、しず、しずか	quiet, calm	36 d

⚥	臆	俺/腎	屋
36 e	♎	♉	♎

With some Trepidation I ordered wine and Kindneys from the Liquor Store.

臆	オク、おしはかる、むね	timidity; heart; fear	臆
臆病	おくびょう	cowardice; timidity	36 e
病	ビョウ、ヘイ、やまい	illness	36 e
俺	エン、おれ	I	俺

127

腎	ジン	kidney	腎
腎臓	じんぞう	kidney	36 e
臓	ゾウ、はらわた	entrails; viscera; bowels	36 e
屋	オク、や	store, building	屋
酒屋	さかや	liquor store	36 e
酒	シュ、さけ、さか	alcohol, sake	36 e

⚗	卸	穏	温
36 f	♎	♉	♎

Wholesale Moderation at the Natural Spring.

卸	おろす、おろし	wholesale, grate	卸
卸売	おろしうり	wholesale	36 f
売	バイ、うる、うれる	sell	36 f
穏	オン、おだ-やか	peace, moderation	穏
穏和	おんわ	moderation	36 f
和	ワ、オ、やわらぐ	Japan, peace, soft	36 f
温	オン、あたたか、あたたかい	warm	温
温泉	おんせん	spa	36 f
泉	セン、いずみ	spring	36 f

⚗	何	夏	仮
36 g	♎	♉	♎

How Many Months ago was the Summer Festival of Pseudonyms?

何	カ、なに、なん	what, how many	何
何ヶ月	なんかげつ	how many months	36 g
月	ゲツ、ガツ、つき	moon	36 g
夏	カ、ゲ、なつ	summer	夏
夏祭	なつまつり	summer festival	36 g
祭	サイ、まつる、まつり	festival, worship	36 g
仮	カ、ケ、かり	temporary, false	仮
仮名	かめい	alias, pseudonym	36 g

名	メイ、ミョウ、な	name, fame	36 g

θ 37 a	嫁 ♎	架 ♉	暇 ♎

The Bride likes to build Bookshelves in her Free Time.

嫁	カ、よめ、とつぐ	marry, bride	嫁
花嫁	はなよめ	bride	37 a
花	カ、はな	flower, blossom	37 a
架	カ、かける、かかる	build, span, frame	架
書架	しょか	bookshelf	37 a
書	ショ、かく	write	37 a
暇	カ、ひま	leisure, free time	暇
余暇	よか	leisure	37 a
余	ヨ、あまる、あます	excess, ample, I	37 a

θ 37 b	箇 ♎	荷 ♉	稼 ♎

Seven financial Burdens require at least a Dual Income.

箇	カ、コ	item (counter)	箇
七箇	ななこ	seven items	37 b
七	シチ、なな、ななつ、なの	seven	37 b
荷	カ、に	load, burden	荷
脚荷	あしに	ballast	37 b
脚	キャク、キャ、あし	leg, foot	37 b
稼	カ、かせぐ	work, earn money	稼
共稼ぎ	ともかせぎ	dual income	37 b
共	キョウ、とも	together	37 b

θ 37 c	渦 ♎	華 ♉	我 ♎

A Vortex of Splendour is whirling in My Heart.

渦	カ、うず	whirlpool, eddy	渦
渦巻き	うずまき	eddy, vortex	37 c
巻	カン、まく、まき	roll, reel, volume	37 c
華	カ、ケ、はな	flower, showy, China	華
華麗	かれい	splendid, magnificent	37 c
麗	レイ、うるわしい	beautiful	37 c
我	ガ、われ、わ	I, self, my	我
我が心	わがこころ	my heart	37 c
心	シン、こころ	heart, feelings	37 c

θ	塊	牙	芽
37 d	♎	♉	♎

Gold Bullion makes Ivory Towers Sprout.

塊	カイ、かたまり	lump, clod, mass	塊
金塊	きんかい	gold bullion	37 d
金	キン、コン、かね	gold, money, metal	37 d
牙	ガ、ゲ、きば	tusk; fang	牙
象牙の塔	ぞうげのとう	ivory tower	37 d
象	ショウ、ゾウ	elephant, image	37 d
塔	トウ	tower, monument	37 d
芽	ガ、め	bud, sprout, shoot	芽
芽生える	めばえる	bud, sprout	37 d
生	セイ、ショウ、いきる	life, birth, grow	37 d

θ	悔	壊	怪
37 e	♎	♉	♎

Regrettably, sunlight Destroyed my favourite Ghost Story.

悔	カイ、くいる、くやむ	regret, repent, vexed	悔
悔恨	かいこん	regret	37 e
恨	コン、うらむ、うらめしい	resent, regret	37 e
壊	カイ、こわす、こわれる	break, destroy, ruin	壊

壊滅	かいめつ	destruction	37 e
滅	メツ、ほろびる、ほろぼす	destroy	37 e
怪	カイ、あやしい、あやしむ	weird, suspicious	怪
怪談	かいだん	ghost story	37 e
談	ダン	conversation, talk	37 e

θ	懐	皆	戒
37 f	♎	♉	♎

After Idleness All must submit to Penance.

懐	カイ、ふところ、なつかしい	bosom, yearn	懐
懐手	ふところで	idleness	37 f
手	シュ、て、た	hand	37 f
皆	カイ、みな	all, everyone, full	皆
皆様	みなさま	everyone	37 f
様	ヨウ、さま	esq.; way; manner	37 f
戒	カイ、いましめる	command	戒
戒行	かいぎょう	penance	37 f
行	コウ、ギョウ、アン、いく	go, conduct	37 f

θ	崖	蓋	絵
37 g	♎	♉	♎

A Palisade with Skulls and Rough Sketches.

崖	ガイ、がけ	cliff; bluff; precipice	崖
断崖	だんがい	palisade; cliff	37 g
断	ダン、たつ、ことわる	cut, decline, judge	37 g
蓋	ガイ、おおう、かさ	cover; lid; flap	蓋
頭蓋骨	ずがいこつ	skull	37 g
頭	トウ、ズ、ト、あたま	head, counter	37 g
骨	コツ、ほね	bone, frame	37 g
絵	カイ、エ	picture	絵
下絵	したえ	rough sketch, cartoon	37 g

下	カ、ゲ、した、もと	base, under, lower	37 g

①	角	柿	骸
38 a	♎	♉	♎

On the Street Corner stood a Reddish-Brown Skeleton.

角	カク、かど、つの	horn, angle	角
街角	まちかど	street corner	38 a
街	ガイ、カイ、まち	road, town, area	38 a
柿	シ、かき	persimmon; shingle	柿
柿色	かきいろ	reddish-brown	38 a
色	ショク、シキ、いろ	colour, sensuality	38 a
骸	ガイ カイ むくろ	bone; body; corpse	骸
骸骨	がいこつ	skeleton	38 a
骨	コツ、ほね	bone, frame	38 a

①	確	格	獲
38 b	♎	♉	♎

Confirming a Genuine Seizure.

確	カク、たしか、たしかめる	ascertain, firm	確
確認	かくにん	confirmation	38 b
認	ニン、みとめる	recognise	38 b
格	カク、コウ	standard, status	格
本格	ほんかく	orthodox, genuine	38 b
本	ホン、もと	root, true, book	38 b
獲	カク、える	obtain, gain, seize	獲
捕獲	ほかく	seizure	38 b
捕	ホ、とらえる、とらわれる	seize, capture	38 b

①	革	隔	覚
38 c	♎	♉	♎

Reforming and Respacing a Sense of Smell.

革	カク、かわ	leather, reform	革
改革	かいかく	reform	38 c
改	カイ、あらためる	reform	38 c
隔	カク、へだてる、ひだたる	separate, interpose	隔
間隔	かんかく	spacing	38 c
間	カン、ケン、あいだ、ま	space, gap	38 c
覚	カク、おぼえる、さます	remember, learn	覚
嗅覚	きゅうかく	sense of smell	38 c
嗅	キュウ かぐ	smell; sniff; scent	38 c

⊕	掛	岳	顎
38 d	♎	♉	♎

Toadies with Imposing Jawbones.

掛	カイ、かける、かかる	be connected, hang	掛
掛かり人	かかりびと	hanger-on	38 d
人	ジン、ニン、ひと	person	38 d
岳	ガク、たけ	peak, imposing	岳
山岳	さんがく	mountains	38 d
山	サン、やま	mountain	38 d
顎	ガク、あご、あぎと	jaw; chin; gill	顎
顎骨	あごぼね; がっこつ	jawbone	38 d
骨	コツ、ほね	bone, frame	38 d

⊕	渇	滑	割
38 e	♎	♉	♎

Thirsting for Slippery Discounts.

渇	カツ、かわく	thirst, parched	渇
渇愛	かつあい	thirst; craving	38 e
愛	アイ	love	38 e
滑	カツ、すべる、なめらか	slide, slip, smooth	滑
潤滑	じゅんかつ	lubrication	38 e

潤	ジュン、うるおう、うるおす	moisten, enrich	38 e
割	カツ、わる、われる、さく	divide, rate	割
割引	わりびき	discount	38 e
引	イン、ひ-く、ひける	pull, draw	38 e

①	葛	釜	鎌
38 f	♎	♉	♎

Trouble in the Boiler Room was settled with a Sickle-Shaped Object.

葛	カツ、くず、つづら	arrowroot; kudzu	葛
葛藤	かっとう	conflict; complication	38 f
藤	トウ、ふじ	wisteria	38 f
釜	フ、かま	kettle; cauldron	釜
釜場	かまば	boiler room	38 f
場	ジョウ、ば	place	38 f
鎌	レン、かま	sickle; scythe; trick	鎌
鎌形	かまがた	sickle-shaped	38 f
形	ケイ、ギョウ、かたち	shape, pattern	38 f

①	寒	堪	瓦
38 g	♎	♉	♎

In a Time of Extreme Cold Patience can Fall Apart.

寒	カン、さむい	cold, midwinter	寒
大寒	だいかん	extreme cold	38 g
大	ダイ、タイ、おおきい	big	38 g
堪	カン、たえる	endure, withstand	堪
堪忍	かんにん	patience	38 g
忍	ニン、しのぶ、しのばせる	endure, stealth	38 g
瓦	ガ、グラム、かわら	tile	瓦
瓦解	がかい	collapse; downfall	38 g
解	カイ、ゲ、とく、とかす	explain, solve	38 g

⊕	幹	換	慣
39 a	♎	♉	♎

Managing the Ventilation Habit.

幹	カン、みき	trunk, main	幹
幹事	かんじ	manager	39 a
事	ジ、ズ、こと	thing, matter, act	39 a
換	カン、かえる、かわる	exchange	換
換気	かんき	ventilation	39 a
気	キ、ケ	spirit	39 a
慣	カン、なれる、ならす	become used to	慣
習慣	しゅうかん	habit, custom	39 a
習	シュウ、ならう	learn, train	39 a

⊕	緩	汗	甘
39 b	♎	♉	♎

In Case of Emergency, apply Sweating Sugar Beet.

緩	カン、ゆるい、ゆるやか	loose, easy, slack	緩
緩急	かんきゅう	in case of emergency	39 b
急	キュウ、いそぐ	emergency, sudden	39 b
汗	カン、あせ	sweat	汗
発汗	はっかん	sweating	39 b
発	ハツ、ホツ	discharge, start, leave	39 b
甘	カン、あまい、あまえる	sweet, presume upon	甘
甘菜	かんさい	sugar beet	39 b
菜	サイ、な	vegetable, rape	39 b

⊕	肝	貫	鑑
39 c	♎	♉	♎

Courage and Penetrating Judgment.

肝	カン、きも	liver, courage	肝
肝っ玉	きもったま	guts, pluck	39 c
玉	ギョク、たま	ball, sphere, coin	39 c
貫	カン、つらぬく	pierce	貫
貫通	かんつう	penetration	39 c
通	ツウ、ツ、とおる	pass, way, commute	39 c
鑑	カン かんがみる	take note, heed	鑑
鑑識	かんしき	judgment; discernment	39 c
識	シキ	knowledge	39 c

⊕	含	関	薬
39 d	♎	♉	♎

Keeping in Mind the Kansai Capsule connection.

含	ガン、ふくむ	include, contain	含
含み置く	ふくみおく	to keep in mind	39 d
置	チ、おく	put, place	39 d
関	カン、せき	connection	関
関西	かんさい	Kansai (SW Japan)	39 d
西	セイ、サイ、にし	west	39 d
薬	ヤク、くすり	medicine, drug	薬
丸薬	がんやく	pill	39 d
丸	ガン、まる、まるい	circle, ship's mark	39 d

⊕	願	玩	企
39 e	♎	♉	♎

Praying for Pleasurable Planning.

願	ガン、ねがう	request, wish	願
願い事	ねがいごと	prayer	39 e
事	ジ、ズ、こと	thing, matter, act	39 e
玩	ガン、もてあそぶ	play; trifle with	玩
愛玩	あいがん	cherish	39 e

愛	アイ	love	39 e
企	キ、くわだてる	plan, undertake	企
企画	きかく	planning; plan; project	39 e
画	ガ、カク	picture, stroke	39 e

⊕	幾	基	伎
39 f	♎	♉	♎

An Enduring Basis for Ability.

幾	キ、いく	how many/much	幾
幾久しく	いくひさしく	forever; eternally	39 f
久	キュウ、ク、ひさしい	long time	39 f
基	キ、もと、もとい	base	基
基礎	きそ	basis	39 f
礎	ソ、いしずえ	foundation stone	39 f
伎	ギ、わざ	deed; skill	伎
技量	ぎりょう	ability; competency	39 f
量	リョウ、はかる	measure, quantity	39 f

⊕	旗	机	忌
39 g	♎	♉	♎

The Flag On the Desk was at Half-Mast.

旗	キ、はた	flag	旗
国旗	こっき	national flag	39 g
国	コク、くに	country, region	39 g
机	キ、つくえ	desk, table	机
机上	きじょう	on the desk	39 g
上	ジョウ、ショウ、うえ、うわ	up, top, go up	39 g
忌	キ、いむ、いまわしい	mourn, odious	忌
忌中	きちゅう	mourning	39 g
中	チュウ、なか	middle, China	39 g

⊕	帰	畿	祈
40 a	♎	♉	♎

Returning from Kinki on a wing and a Prayer.

帰	キ、かえる	return	帰
帰り道	かえりみち	way back	40 a
道	ドウ、トウ、みち	way, road	40 a
畿	キ、みやこ	capital; suburbs of capital	畿
近畿	きんき	Kinki (Osaka, Kyoto, Nara)	40 a
近	キン、ちかい	near	40 a
祈	キ、いのる	pray, hope	祈
祈念	きねん	prayer	40 a
念	ネン	thought, concern	40 a

⊕	貴	輝	飢
40 b	♎	♉	♎

Precious little Light during Hunger and Cold.

貴	キ、たっとい、とうとい	precious, revered	貴
貴重	きちょうな	precious	40 b
重	ジュウ、チョウ、え、おもい	heavy, pile, -fold	40 b
輝	キ、かがやく	sparkle, shine	輝
輝度	きど	brightness	40 b
度	ド、ト、タク、たび	degree, times	40 b
飢	キ、うえる	starve, hunger	飢
飢寒	きかん	hunger and cold	40 b
寒	カン、さむい	cold, midwinter	40 b

⊕	宜	亀	偽
40 c	♎	♉	♎

A good Opportunity to start Cracking with the Counterfeit Paper Money.

宜	ギ、よろしい	good, right	宜
機宜	きぎ	opportunity; occasion	40 c
機	キ、はた	loom, device, occasion	40 c
亀	キ、かめ	turtle	亀
亀裂	きれつ	crack; crevice; fissure	40 c
裂	レツ、さく、さける	split, rend, rip	40 c
偽	ギ、いつわる、にせ	false, lie	偽
偽札	にせさつ	counterfeit paper money	40 c
札	サツ、ふだ	paper money, note	40 c

⊕	戯	疑	吉
40 d	♎	♉	♎

A Caricatural and Suspicious Bad Portent.

戯	ギ、たわむれる	play, frolic, joke	戯
戯画	ぎが	caricature	40 d
画	ガ、カク	picture, stroke	40 d
疑	ギ、うたがう	doubt, suspect	疑
疑問	ぎもん	doubt	40 d
問	モン、とう、とい、とん	ask	40 d
吉	キチ、キツ	good luck, joy	吉
不吉	ふきつ	bad omen	40 d
不	フ、ブ	not, un-, dis-	40 d

⊕	逆	虐	詰
40 e	♎	♉	♎

The Traitor underwent Cruel Cross-Examination.

逆	ギャク、さか、さからう	reverse, oppose	逆
反逆	はんぎゃく	treason	40 e
反	ハン、ホン、タン、そる	oppose, anti, reverse	40 e
虐	ギャク、しいたげる	cruelty, oppress	虐
残虐	ざんぎゃく	cruelty	40 e

残	ザン、のこる、のこす	leave, cruel, harm	40 e
詰	キツ、つめる、つまる	pack, packed, full	詰
詰問	きつもん	cross-examination	40 e
問	モン、とう、とい、とん	ask	40 e

⊕	臼	丘	息
40 f	♎	♉	♎

Climbing up Molar Hill for some Rest and recreation.

臼	キュウ、うす	mortar	臼
臼歯	きゅうし	molar	40 f
歯	シ、は	tooth	40 f
丘	キュウ、おか	hill	丘
丘陵	きゅうりょう	hill, hillock	40 f
陵	リョウ、みささぎ	imperial tomb, mound	40 f
息	ソク、いき	breath, rest, child	息
休息	きゅうそく	rest	40 f
休	キュウ、やすむ	rest	40 f

⊕	朽	吸	弓
40 g	♎	♉	♎

The Decaying Vampire Took a Bow.

朽	キュウ、くちる	decay, rot	朽
朽ち葉	くちば	dead leaves	40 g
葉	ヨウ、は	leaf	40 g
吸	キュウ、すう	suck, inhale	吸
吸血鬼	きゅうけつき	vampire	40 g
血	ケツ、ち	blood	40 g
弓	キュウ、ゆみ	bow	弓
弓道	きゅうどう	archery	40 g
道	ドウ、トウ、みち	way, road	40 g

⊕	究	泣	球
41 a	♎	♉	♎

Investigating a Weeping Bulb.

究	キュウ、きわめる	investigate	究
研究	けんきゅう	research	41 a
研	ケン、とぐ	hone, refine	41 a
泣	キュウ、なく	weep, cry	泣
泣き出す	なきだす	burst into tears	41 a
出	シュツ、でる、だす	emerge, put out	41 a
球	キュウ、たま	sphere, ball	球
球茎	きゅうけい	bulb	41 a
茎	ケイ、くき	stalk, stem	41 a

⊕	去	牛	居
41 b	♎	♉	♎

Last Year a Heifer came into the Palace.

去	キョ、コ、さる	go, leave, past	去
去年	きょねん	last year	41 b
年	ネン、とし	year	41 b
牛	ギュウ、うし	cow	牛
雌牛	めうし	cow, heifer	41 b
雌	シ、め、めす	female	41 b
居	キョ、いる	be, reside	居
皇居	こうきょ	Imperial Palace	41 b
皇	コウ、オウ	emperor	41 b

⊕	挙	拠	拒
41 c	♎	♉	♎

Second Attempt at a Base Denial.

挙	キョ、あげる、あがる	offer, raise, act, perform	挙
再挙	さいきょ	second attempt	41 c
再	サイ、サ、ふたたび	again, twice, re-	41 c
拠	キョ	base, basis	拠
根拠	こんきょ	base, basis	41 c
根	コン、ね	root, base	41 c
拒	キョ、こばむ	refuse, resist	拒
拒否	きょひ	denial	41 c
否	ヒ、いな	no, decline, deny	41 c

⊕	虚	漁	魚
41 d	♎	♉	♎

Conceited Fishers and narcistic Fish.

虚	キョ、コ	empty, hollow, dip	虚
虚栄	きょえい	vanity	41 d
栄	エイ、さかえる、はえる	flourish	41 d
漁	ギョ、リョウ	fishing	漁
漁場	ぎょじょう, りょうば	fishing grounds/banks	41 d
場	ジョウ、ば	place	41 d
魚	ギョ、うお、さかな	fish	魚
魚貝	ぎょかい	marine products; fish	41 d
貝	かい	shellfish	41 d

⊕	叫	京	境
41 e	♎	♉	♎

Screaming at the Tokyo Provincial Boundary.

叫	キョウ、さけぶ	shout, yell	叫
叫喚	きょうかん	cry, scream	41 e
喚	カン	shout, yell	41 e
京	キョウ、ケイ	capital	京
東京	とうきょう	Tokyo	41 e

東	トウ、ひがし	east	41 e
境	キョウ、ケイ、さかい	boundary, border	境
州境	しゅうきょう	provincial boundary	41 e
州	シュウ、す	state, province	41 e

⊕	挟	怖	恭
41 f	♎	♉	♎

No Dilemma between Horror and Obedience.

挟	キョウ、はさむ	insert, pinch	挟
板挟み	いたばさみ	dilemma	41 f
板	ハン、バン、いた	board, plate	41 f
怖	フ、こわい	fear, afraid	怖
恐怖	きょうふ	horror	41 f
恐	キョウ、おそれる	fear, awe	41 f
恭	キョウ、うやうやしい	respectful	恭
恭順	きょうじゅん	obedience	41 f
順	ジュン	sequence, compliance	41 f

⊕	矯	狂	狭
41 g	♎	♉	♎

Straightening Up that Maddingly Cramped doss house.

矯	キョウ、ためる	straighten	矯
矯め直す	ためなおす	correct	41 g
直	チョク、ジキ、なおす	direct, fix	41 g
狂	キョウ、くるおしい	lunatic, mad	狂
荒れ狂う	あれくるう	rage, run amok	41 g
荒	コウ、あらい、あれる	rough, wild	41 g
狭	キョウ、せまい、せばめる	narrow, small	狭
狭苦しい	せまくるしい	cramped	41 g
苦	ク、くるしい、くるしむ	painful, bitter	41 g

♉	脅	胸	興
42 a	♎	♉	♎

Threatening Chest Hair Raised Excitement.

脅	キョウ、おびやかす、おどす	threaten, coerce	脅
脅迫	きょうはく	threat	42 a
迫	ハク、せまる	press, draw near	42 a
胸	キョウ、むね、むな	chest, breast	胸
胸毛	むなげ	chest hair	42 a
毛	モウ、け	hair	42 a
興	コウ、キョウ、おこる	rise, interest	興
興奮	こうふん	get excited	42 a
奮	フン、ふるう	be excited, stir	42 a

♉	驚	響	郷
42 b	♎	♉	♎

Wonderful Echoes of Homesickness.

驚	キョウ、おどろく	surprise	驚
驚異	きょうい	miracle, wonder	42 b
異	イ、こと	differ, strange	42 b
響	キョウ、ひびく	resound, echo, effect	響
響き渡る	ひびきわたる	resound	42 b
渡	ト、わたる、わたす	cross, hand over	42 b
郷	キョウ、ゴウ	village, rural	郷
望郷	ぼうきょう	homesickness	42 b
望	ボウ、モウ、のぞむ	wish, hope, gaze	42 b

♉	仰	凝	暁
42 c	♎	♉	♎

Looking Up to Stare at Venus.

仰	ギョウ、コウ、あおぐ	look up, state, respect	仰
信仰	しんこう	faith, creed	42 c
信	シン	trust, believe	42 c
凝	ギョウ、こる、こらす	stiff, engrossed, elaborate	凝
凝視	ぎょうし	stare	42 c
視	シ	see, look, regard	42 c
暁	ギョウ、あかつき	dawn, light, event	暁
暁星	ぎょうせい	Venus, rarity	42 c
星	セイ、ショウ、ほし	star	42 c

| ♉ | 極 | 僅 | 曲 |
| 42 d | ♎ | ♉ | ♎ |

That South Pole is a Little Bent.

極	キョク、ゴク、きわめる	extreme, pole	極
南極	なんきょく	South Pole	42 d
南	ナン、ナ、みなみ	south	42 d
僅	キン、わずか	a wee bit	僅
僅差	きんさ	narrow margin	42 d
差	サ、さす	difference, thrust	42 d
曲	キョク、まがる、まげる	bend, melody	曲
曲線	きょくせん	curve	42 d
線	セン	line	42 d

| ♉ | 勤 | 錦 | 巾 |
| 42 e | ♎ | ♉ | ♎ |

Working the Brocade Dust Cloth.

勤	キン、ゴン、つとめる	work, duties	勤
出勤	しゅっきん	attendance	42 e
出	シュツ、スイ、でる、だす	emerge, put out	42 e
錦	キン、にしき	brocade	錦
錦絵	にしきえ	woodblock print	42 e

絵	カイ、エ	picture	42 e
巾	キン、はば	towel; width	巾
雑巾	ぞうきん	house-cloth	42 e
雑	ザツ、ゾウ	miscellany	42 e

☿	襟	謹	琴
42 f	♎	♉	♎

From the Nape of the Neck to the Serious Heartstrings.

襟	キン、えり	collar, neck, heart	襟
襟首	えりくび	nape of the neck	42 f
首	シュ、くび	head, neck, chief	42 f
謹	キン、つつしむ	circumspect	謹
謹厳	きんげん	seriousness	42 f
厳	ゲン、ゴン、きびしい	severe, strict	42 f
琴	キン、こと	koto	琴
琴線	きんせん	heartstrings	42 f
線	セン	line	42 f

☿	駆	九	駒
42 g	♎	♉	♎

Running around the Bend across the Small Fence.

駆	ク、かける、かる	gallop, spur on	駆
駆け回る	かけまわる	to run about	42 g
回	カイ、エ、まわる	turn, rotate	42 g
九	キュウ、ク、ここの	nine	九
九折	きゅうせつ	many turns (road)	42 g
折	セツ、おる、り、おれる	bend, break	42 g
駒	ク、こま	horse; colt	駒
駒寄せ	こまよせ	small fence	42 g
寄	キ、よる、よせる	draw near, visit	42 g

	36	37	38	39	40	41	42
a	縁起	花嫁	街角	幹事	帰り道	研究	脅迫
	鉛筆	書架	柿色	換気	近畿	泣き出す	胸毛
	妖艶	余暇	骸骨	習慣	祈念	球茎	興奮
b	汚れ物	七箇	確認	緩急	貴重	去年	驚異
	塩水	脚荷	本格	発汗	輝度	雌牛	響き渡る
	凹眼	共稼ぎ	捕獲	甘菜	飢寒	皇居	望郷
c	旺盛	渦巻き	改革	肝っ玉	機宜	再挙	信仰
	手押し車	華麗	間隔	貫通	亀裂	根拠	凝視
	奥底	我が心	嗅覚	鑑識	偽札	拒否	暁星
d	横顔	金塊	掛かり人	含み置く	戯画	虚栄	南極
	黄色	象牙の塔	山岳	関西	疑問	漁場	僅差
	静岡	芽生える	顎骨	丸薬	不吉	魚貝	曲線
e	臆病	悔恨	渇愛	願い事	反逆	叫喚	出勤
*	俺 腎臓	壊滅	潤滑	愛玩	残虐	東京	錦絵
	酒屋	怪談	割引	企画	詰問	州境	雑巾
f	卸売	懐手	葛藤	幾久しく	臼歯	板挟み	襟首
	穏和	皆様	釜場	基礎	丘陵	恐怖	謹厳
	温泉	戒行	鎌形	技量	休息	恭順	琴線
g	何ヶ月	断崖	大寒	国旗	朽ち葉	矯め直す	駆け回る
	夏祭	頭蓋骨	堪忍	机上	吸血鬼	荒れ狂う	九折
	仮名	下絵	瓦解	忌中	弓道	狭苦しい	駒寄せ

CHAPTER 7
Weeks 43 – 49

	愚	虞	隅
43 a	♎	♉	♎

The Foolish lad was Likely to Commit a Crime on the Corner.

愚	グ、おろか	foolish	愚
愚劣	ぐれつ	foolishness; stupidity	43 a
劣	レツ、おとる	be inferior	43 a
虞	ぐ、おそれ	fear, anxiety	虞
虞犯	ぐはん	likely to cmt. a crime	43 a
犯	ハン、おかす	crime, commit	43 a
隅	グウ、すみ	corner, nook	隅
隅石	すみいし	cornerstone	43 a
石	セキ、シャク、コク、いし	stone, rock	43 a

	掘	串	窟
43 b	♎	♉	♉

Unearthing an ancient Skewer from the Grotto.

掘	クツ、ほる	dig	掘
掘り出す	ほりだす	unearth	43 b
出	シュツ、でる、だす	emerge, put out	43 b
串	カン、セン、くし	skewer, kebab	串
串刺し	くしざし	skewer	43 b
刺	シ、さす、ささる	pierce, stab, thorn	43 b
窟	クツ、あな、いわや	cavern	窟
岩屋	いわや	cavern; grotto	43 b
岩	ガン、いわ	rock, crag	43 b

	熊	靴	桑
43 c	♎	♉	♎

Bear in Boots Damaged a Mulberry Field.

熊	ユウ、くま	bear	熊
熊害	ゆうがい	damages caused by bears	43 c
害	ガイ	harm, damage	43 c
靴	カ、くつ	shoe	靴
長靴	ながぐつ	boot	43 c
長	チョウ、ながい	long, senior	43 c
桑	ソウ、くわ	mulberry	桑
桑原	くわばら	mulberry field	43 c
原	ゲン、はら	plain, origin	43 c

| ✧ | 群 | 薫 | 君 |
| 43 d | ♎ | ♉ | ♎ |

Crowds flocked to the Fragrant Lord.

群	グン、むれる、むれ、むら	group, flock	群
群衆	ぐんしゅう	crowd, multitude	43 d
衆	シュウ、シュ	multitude, populace	43 d
薫	クン、かおる	aroma, fragrance	薫
薫香	くんこう	insense	43 d
香	コウ、キョウ、か、かおり	fragrance, incense	43 d
君	クン、きみ	lord, you mr	君
君主	くんしゅ	ruler, monarch	43 d
主	シュ、ス、ぬし、おも	master, owner, main	43 d

| ✧ | 係 | 傾 | 兄 |
| 43 e | ♎ | ♉ | ♎ |

The Clerk in Charge was Inclined to turn to Dicey Brothers.

係	ケイ、かかる、かかり	involvement	係
係員	かかりいん	clerk in charge	43 e
員	イン	member, official	43 e
傾	ケイ、かたむく	incline, dedicate	傾
傾向	けいこう	tendency; trend	43 e

向	コウ、むく、むける	face towards, beyond	43 e
兄	ケイ、キョウ、あに	elder brother	兄
兄弟	きょうだい	brothers	43 e
弟	テイ、ダイ、おとうと	younger brother	43 e

✧	契	恵	息
43 f	♎	♉	♎

Contract for Benevolence and Rest.

契	ケイ、ちぎる	pledge, join	契
契約	けいやく	contract	43 f
約	ヤク	promise, approximately	43 f
恵	ケイ、エ、めぐむ	blessing, kindness	恵
仁恵	じんけい	mercy, benevolence	43 f
仁	ジン、ニ	virtue, benevolence, man	43 f
息	ソク、いき	breath, rest, child	息
休息	きゅうそく	rest	43 f
休	キュウ、やすむ	rest	43 f

✧	掲	敬	提
43 g	♎	♉	♎

A Publication of Acclaimed Cooperation.

掲	ケイ、かかげる	display, hoist, print	掲
掲載	けいさい	publication	43 g
載	サイ、のせる、のる	load, carry	43 g
敬	ケイ、うやまう	respect	敬
尊敬	そんけい	respect	43 g
尊	ソン、たっとい、とうとい	value, esteem, your	43 g
提	テイ、さげる	hold, carry, offer	提
提携	ていけい	cooperation, tie-up	43 g
携	ケイ、たずさえる	carry, participate	43 g

	経	稽	継
44 a	♎	♉	♎

The Economic Practice of Inheritance.

経	ケイ、キョウ、へる	pass, longitude	経
経済	けいざい	economy	44 a
済	サイ、すむ、すます	settle, finish	44 a
稽	ケイ、かんがえる、とどめる	think; consider	稽
稽古	けいこ	practice	44 a
古	コ、ふるい、ふるす	old	44 a
継	ケイ、つぐ	inherit, follow	継
跡継ぎ	あとつぎ	successor, heir	44 a
跡	セキ、あと	trace, remains	44 a

	詣	軽	蛍
44 b	♎	♉	♎

Visiting a Light and Fluorescent Temple.

詣	ケイ、もうでる	visit a temple	詣
参詣	さんけい	visit to a temple	44 b
参	サン、まいる	attend, be in love	44 b
軽	ケイ、かるい、かろやか	light, flippant	軽
軽少	けいしょう	trifling; slight	44 b
少	ショウ、すくない、すこし	a little, few	44 b
蛍	ケイ、ほたる	firefly	蛍
蛍光	けいこう	fluorescence	44 b
光	コウ、ひかる、ひかり	light, shine	44 b

	迎	鯨	鶏
44 c	♎	♉	♎

Greetings with Whale Oil and Eggs.

迎	ゲイ、むかえる	greet, welcome, meet	迎
迎え人	むかえびと	(a) greeter	44 c
人	ジン、ニン、ひと	person	44 c
鯨	ゲイ、くじら	whale	鯨
鯨油	げいゆ	whale oil	44 c
油	ユ、あぶら	oil	44 c
鶏	ケイ、にわとり	chicken, hen, cock	鶏
鶏卵	けいらん	hen's egg	44 c
卵	ラン、たまご	egg, ovum, spawn	44 c

☿	隙	激	撃
44 d	♎	♉	♎

Into the Breach with a Furious Attack.

隙	ゲキ、すき	crevice; fissure	隙
隙間	すきま	crevice; crack; gap	44 d
間	カン、ケン、あいだ、ま	space, gap	44 d
激	ゲキ、はげしい	violent, fierce, strong	激
憤激	ふんげき	fury	44 d
憤	フン、いきどおる	indignant, angry	44 d
撃	ゲキ、うつ	strike, attack, fire	撃
攻撃	こうげき	attack	44 d
攻	コウ、せめる	attack	44 d

☿	欠	潔	桁
44 e	♎	♉	♎

A Shortage of Clean Clothes Racks.

欠	ケツ、かける、かく	lack	欠
欠乏	けつぼう	lack, scarcity, shortage	44 e
乏	ボウ、とぼしい	meager, scanty, scarce	44 e
潔	ケツ、いさぎよい	clean, pure	潔
清潔	せいけつ	cleanliness	44 e

清	セイ、ショウ、きよい	pure, clean	44 e
桁	コウ、けた	beam; girder; spar; unit	桁
衣桁	いこう	clothes rack	44 e
衣	イ、ころも	garment	44 e

☻	兼	穴	剣
44 f	♎	♉	♎

Dual Use of Stopgaps and Bayonets.

兼	ケン、かねる	combine, unable	兼
兼用	けんよう	dual purpose	44 f
用	ヨウ、もちいる	use	44 f
穴	ケツ、あな	hole	穴
穴埋め	あなうめ	stopgap	44 f
埋	マイ、うめる、うまる	bury	44 f
剣	ケン、つるぎ	sword, bayonet	剣
剣舞	けんぶ	sword dance	44 f
舞	ブ、まう、まい	dance, flit	44 f

☻	堅	懸	嫌
44 g	♎	♉	♎

Stronghold of Perilous Loathing.

堅	ケン、かたい	firm, solid, hard	堅
堅陣	けんじん	stronghold	44 g
陣	ジン	position, camp	44 g
懸	ケン、ケ、かける、かかる	attach, hang	懸
命懸け	いのちがけ	perilous	44 g
命	メイ、ミョウ、いのち	life, order	44 g
嫌	ケン、ゲン、きらう、いや	dislike(d)	嫌
嫌悪	けんお	loathing	44 g
悪	アク、オ、わるい	bad, hate	44 g

♣	献	犬	絹
45 a	♎	♉	♎

A Dedicated Watchdog guarded the Silk.

献	ケン、コン	dedicate, present	献
貢献	こうけん	contribution	45 a
貢	コウ、ク、みつぐ	tribute	45 a
犬	ケン、いぬ	dog	犬
番犬	ばんけん	watchdog	45 a
番	バン	turn, number, guard	45 a
絹	ケン、きぬ	silk	絹
絹布	けんぷ	silk; silk cloth	45 a
布	フ、ぬの	cloth, spread	45 a

♣	賢	肩	軒
45 b	♎	♉	♎

The Wise pretend to Shoulder the Five Houses.

賢	ケン、かしこい	wise	賢
賢立つ	かしこだて	pretence of wisdom	45 b
立	リツ、リュウ、たてる	stand, rise, leave	45 b
肩	ケン、かた	shoulder	肩
肩肘	かたひじ	shoulder and elbow	45 b
肘	チュウ、ひじ	elbow; arm	45 b
軒	ケン、のき	eaves, house, counter	軒
五軒	ごけん	five houses	45 b
五	ゴ、いつ、いつつ	five	45 b

♣	験	鍵	険
45 c	♎	♉	♎

Experience Ebenezer Keystroke's bold Adventure.

験	ケン、ゲン	examine	験
経験	けいけん	experience	45 c
経	ケイ、キョウ、へる	pass, sutra, longitude	45 c
鍵	ケン、かぎ	key	鍵
打鍵	だけん	keystroke	45 c
打	ダ、うつ	hit, strike	45 c
険	ケン、けわしい	steep, severe, perilous	険
冒険	ぼうけん	adventure	45 c
冒	ボウ、おかす	defy, risk, attack	45 c

ꙮ	弦	減	幻
45 d	♎	♉	♎

A slack Bowstring Decreases the Magic.

弦	ゲン、つる	(bow)string	弦
弓弦	ゆみずる	bowstring	45 d
弓	キュウ、ゆみ	bow	45 d
減	ゲン、へる、へらす	decrease	減
減少	げんしょう	decrease	45 d
少	ショウ、すくない、すこし	a little, few	45 d
幻	ゲン、まぼろし	illusion, magic	幻
幻術	げんじゅつ	magic	45 d
術	ジュツ	means, technique	45 d

ꙮ	限	源	舷
45 e	♎	♉	♎

Infinite Resources on Starboard.

限	ゲン、かぎる	limit	限
無限	むげん	infinity	45 e
無	ム、ブ、ない	not, non, cease to be	45 e
源	ゲン、みなもと	source, origin	源
資源	しげん	resources	45 e

資	シ	capital, resources	45 e
舷	ゲン、ふなばた	gunwale	舷
右舷	うげん	starboard	45 e
右	ウ、ユウ、みぎ	right	45 e

⚗	固	己	呼
45 f	♎	♉	♎

Insisting on a Selfish Roll Call.

固	コ、かためる、かたまる	hard, firm, solid	固
固執	こしつ	persist in, insist on	45 f
執	シツ、シュウ、とる	take, grasp, execute	45 f
己	コ、キ、おのれ	I, me, you, self	己
自己	じこ	self	45 f
自	ジ、シ、みずから	self	45 f
呼	コ、よぶ	call, breathe	呼
点呼	てんこ	roll call	45 f
点	テン	point, mark	45 f

⚗	枯	庫	故
45 g	♎	♉	♎

Business Conditions are Poor for a Depot with Stolen Goods.

枯	コ、かれる、からす	wither, decay	枯
冬枯れ	ふゆがれ	poor business conditions	45 g
冬	トウ、ふゆ	winter	45 g
庫	コ、ク	storehouse	庫
車庫	しゃこ	garage, depot	45 g
車	シャ、くるま	vehicle, chariot	45 g
故	コ、ゆえ	past, reason	故
故買	こばい	buying stolen goods	45 g
買	バイ、かう	buy	45 g

✄	雇	虎	股
46 a	♎	♉	♎

Employed at the Tiger's Den near the Forked Tree.

雇	コ、やとう	employ, hire	雇
雇い人	やといにん	employee	46 a
人	ジン、ニン、ひと	person	46 a
虎	コ、とら	tiger; drunkard	虎
虎穴	こけつ	tiger's den; dangerous spot	46 a
穴	ケツ、あな	hole	46 a
股	コ、また、もも	thigh; crotch; yarn; strand	股
股木	またぎ	forked tree	46 a
木	ボク、モク、きこ	tree, wood	46 a

✄	顧	互	鼓
46 b	♎	♉	♎

Looking Back at Compromised Drumming.

顧	コ、かえりみる	look back	顧
回顧	かいこ	retrospection	46 b
回	カイ、エ、まわる	turn, rotate	46 b
互	ゴ、たがい	mutual, reciprocal	互
互譲	ごじょう	concession, compromise	46 b
譲	ジョウ、ゆずる	hand over, yield	46 b
鼓	コ、つづみ	drum	鼓
鼓動	こどう	drumming	46 b
動	ドウ、うごく	move	46 b

✄	悟	後	呉
46 c	♎	♉	♎

Understanding comes After Giving.

悟	ゴ、さとる	perceive, discern	悟
悟性	ごせい	wisdom	46 c
性	セイ、ショウ	nature, sex	46 c
後	ゴ、コウ、のち、うしろ	behind, after	後
後盾	うしろだて	backing	46 c
盾	ジュン、たて	shield, pretext	46 c
呉	ゴ くれる	give, Wu China	呉
呉れ手	くれて	donor	46 c
手	シュ、て、た	hand	46 c

✠	功	乞	効
46 d	♎	♉	♎

Successful Supplicants savour Sufficiency.

功	コウ、ク	merit, service	功
成功	せいこう	success	46 d
成	セイ、ジョウ、なる、なす	become, make	46 d
乞	コツ、キツ、キ、こう	beg; invite; ask	乞
乞食	こじき	beggar	46 d
食	ショク、ジキ、くう、たべる	food, eat	46 d
効	コウ、き-く	effect, efficacy	効
有効	ゆうこうな	valid	46 d
有	ユウ、ウ、ある	have, exist	46 d

✠	厚	勾	口
46 e	♎	♉	♎

The Audacious burglar was Arrested before a broken Window.

厚	コウ、あつい	thick, kind	厚
厚顔	こうがん	impudence; audacity	46 e
顔	ガン、かお	face	46 e
勾	コウ、かぎ	be bent; slope; capture	勾
勾引	こういん	arrest; custody; abduction	46 e

160

引	イン、ひく、ひける	pull, draw	46 e
口	コウ、ク、くち	mouth, opening	口
窓口	まどぐち	window	46 e
窓	ソウ、まど	window	46 e

✗	好	巧	工
46 f	♎	♉	♎

Friendly and Skilful Carpenters.

好	コウ、このむ、すく	like, good, fine	好
修好	しゅうこう	amity, friendship	46 f
修	シュウ、シュ、おさめる	practice, master	46 f
巧	コウ、たくみ	skill	巧
技巧	ぎこう	skill	46 f
技	ギ、わざ	craft, skill	46 f
工	コウ、ク	work	工
大工	だいく	carpenter	46 f
大	ダイ、タイ、おお、おおきい	big	46 f

✗	広	幸	慌
46 g	♎	♉	♎

Advertising for Jovial Blunderers.

広	コウ、ひろい、ひろまる	wide, spacious	広
広告	こうこく	advertisement	46 g
告	コク、つげる	proclaim, inform	46 g
幸	コウ、さいわい、しあわせ	happiness, luck	幸
幸福	こうふく	happiness	46 g
福	フク	good fortune	46 g
慌	コウ、あわてる	be flustered	慌
慌て者	あわたもの	blunderer	46 g
者	シャ、もの	person	46 g

⚱	構	梗	控
47 a	♎	♉	♎

Mental Readiness Stopped in the Waiting Room.

構	コウ、かまえる、かまう	build, mind	構
心構え	こころがまえ	mental readiness	47 a
心	シン、こころ	heart, feelings	47 a
梗	コウ、キョウ、やまにれ	for the most part	梗
梗塞	こうそく	stoppage; blocking	47 a
塞	サイ、ソク、とりで	close	47 a
控	コウ、ひかえる	write down, wait	控
控え所	ひかえじょ	waiting room	47 a
所	ショ、ところ	place, situation	47 a

⚱	江	硬	溝
47 b	♎	♉	♎

Creek water Hardened to Ditch Mud.

江	コウ、え	inlet, river	江
入り江	いりえ	creek, inlet	47 b
入	ニュウ、いる、いれる	to get in, to flow in	47 b
硬	コウ、かたい	hard	硬
硬化	こうか	hardening	47 b
化	カ、ケ、ばける、ばかす	change, bewitch	47 b
溝	コウ、みぞ	ditch, channel	溝
溝泥	どぶどろ	ditch mud	47 b
泥	デイ、どろ	mud, adhere to	47 b

⚱	絞	耕	綱
47 c	♎	♉	♎

Don't Strangle Farming's Main Principles.

絞	コウ、しぼる、しめる	strangle, wring	絞
絞め殺す	しめころす	strangle	47 c
殺	サツ、サイ、セツ、ころす	kill	47 c
耕	コウ、たがやす	till, plow	耕
耕作	こうさく	farming	47 c
作	サク、サ、つくる	make	47 c
綱	コウ、つな	line, principle	綱
大綱	たいこう	main principles	47 c
大	ダイ、タイ、おおきい	big	47 c

♎	降	鋼	考
47 d	♎	♉	♎

Getting On and Off on Steely Ideas.

降	コウ、おりる、ふる	fall, descend	降
乗り降り	のりおり	get on and off	47 d
乗	ジョウ、のる、のせる	ride, mount	47 d
鋼	コウ、はがね	steel	鋼
鋼鉄	こうてつ	steel	47 d
鉄	テツ	iron, steel	47 d
考	コウ、かんがえる	consider	考
考案	こうあん	idea	47 d
案	アン	plan	47 d

♎	刻	腰	合
47 e	♎	♉	♎

High Time for Hip Choral Groups.

刻	コク、きざむ	chop, mince, engrave	刻
時刻	じこく	time, hour	47 e
時	ジ、とき	time	47 e
腰	ヨウ、こし	hip, lower back	腰
物腰	ものごし	manner	47 e

物	ブツ、モツ、もの	thing	47 e
合	ゴウ、ガッ、カッ、あう	meet, join, fit	合
合唱	がっしょう	chorus	47 e
唱	ショウ、となえる	recite, preach	47 e

☖	込	頃	困
47 f	♎	♉	♎

Applied for Recent Poverty.

込	こむ、こめる	put in, be crowded	込
申し込む	もうしこむ	apply	47 f
申	シン、もうす	say, expound	47 f
頃	ケイ、ころ	time; about; toward	頃
日頃	ひごろ	recently	47 f
日	ニチ、ジツ、ひ、か	sun, day	47 f
困	コン、こまる	quandary, annoyed	困
貧困	ひんこん	poverty	47 f
貧	ヒン、ビン、まずしい	poor, meagre	47 f

☖	痕	混	懇
47 g	♎	♉	♎

Scars of many Confusing Conversations.

痕	コン、あと	mark; foot print	痕
傷痕	きずあと	scar	47 g
傷	ショウ、きず、いたむ	wound, injury	47 g
混	コン、まじる、まざる	mix, confusion	混
混乱	こんらん	confusion	47 g
乱	ラン、みだれる、みだす	disorder, riot	47 g
懇	コン、ねんごろ	courtesy, cordiality	懇
懇談	こんだん	chat	47 g
談	ダン	conversation, talk	47 g

δ	唆	魂	左
48 a	♎	♉	♎

Enticing Salesmanship from the Left.

唆	サ、そそのかす	entice, incite	唆
教唆	きょうさ	incitement	48 a
教	キョウ、おしえる、おそわる	teach	48 a
魂	コン、たましい	soul, spirit	魂
商魂	しょうこん	salesmanship	48 a
商	ショウ、あきなう	trade, deal, sell	48 a
左	サ、ひだり	left	左
左側	ひだりがわ	leftside	48 a
側	ソク、かわ	side	48 a

δ	催	挫	鎖
48 b	♎	♉	♎

Demanding an end to the Frustrating Blockade.

催	サイ、もよおす	organise, muster	催
催促	さいそく	request; demand	48 b
促	ソク、うながす	urge, press	48 b
挫	ザ、サ、くじく、くじける	crush; break; sprain	挫
挫折	ざせつ	frustration	48 b
折	セツ、おる、おり、おれる	bend, break	48 b
鎖	サ、くさり	close, shut, chain	鎖
封鎖	ふうさ	blockade, freeze	48 b
封	フウホウ	close off, fief	48 b

δ	妻	最	彩
48 c	♎	♉	♎

Consorts with the Highest Colour.

妻	サイ、つま	wife	妻
夫妻	ふさい	husband and wife	48 c
夫	フ、フウ、おっと	husband, man	48 c
最	サイ、もっとも	most, -est	最
高最	こうさい	highest	48 c
高	コウ、たかい、たかまる	tall, high, sum	48 c
彩	サイ、いろどる	colour	彩
色彩	しきさい	colouring	48 c
色	ショク、シキ、いろ	colour, sensuality	48 c

ð	採	歳	砕
48 d	♎	♉	♎

Harvesting Two Year Old Icebreakers.

採	サイ、とる	take, gather	採
採取	さいしゅ	harvesting	48 d
取	シュ、とる	take control	48 d
歳	サイセイ	year	歳
二歳	にさい	two years old	48 d
二	ニ、ふた、ふたつ	two	48 d
砕	サイ、くだく、くだける	break, smash	砕
砕氷船	さいひょうせん	icebreaker	48 d
氷	ヒョウ、こおり、ひ	ice, hail, freeze	48 d
船	セン、ふね、ふな	boat, ship	48 d

ð	裁	際	在
48 e	♎	♉	♎

Trialing International Sojourns.

裁	サイ、たつ、さばく	judge, decide, cut	裁
裁判	さいばん	trial	48 e
判	ハン、バン	seal; stamp; judgement	48 e
際	サイ、きわ	occasion, edge, contact	際

国際	こくさい	international	48 e
国	コク、くに	country, region	48 e
在	ザイ、ある	exist, outskirts, suburbs	在
滞在	たいざい	sojourn, stay	48 e
滞	タイ、とどこおる	stop, stagnate	48 e

♅	坂	罪	阪
48 f	♎	♉	♎

Steep Roads lead to Sinful Osaka and Kobe.

坂	ハン、さか	slope	坂
坂道	さかみち	hill road	48 f
道	ドウ、トウ、みち	way, road	48 f
罪	ザイ、つみ	crime, sin	罪
罪深い	つみぶかい	sinful	48 f
深	シン、ふかい、ふかまる	deep, deepen	48 f
阪	ハン、さか	heights; slope	阪
阪神	はんしん	Osaka and Kobe	48 f
神	シン、ジン、かみ、かん	god, spirit	48 f

♅	削	搾	埼
48 g	♎	♉	♎

Reducing Exploitation in Saitama Prefecture.

削	サク、けずる	pare, reduce	削
削除	さくじょ	deletion	48 g
除	ジョ、ジ、のぞく	exlude, remove	48 g
搾	サク、しぼる	wring, press	搾
搾取	さくしゅ	exploitation	48 g
取	シュ、とる	take control	48 g
埼	キ、さい、さき	cape; spit; promontory	埼
埼玉県	さいたまけん	Saitama Prefecture	48 g
玉	ギョク、たま	ball, sphere, coin	48 g

県	ケン	prefecture	48 g

☿	冊	桜	刷
49 a	♎	♉	♎

Two Volumes of Ephemeral Printed works.

冊	サツ、サク	book, volume	冊
二冊	にさつ	two volumes	49 a
二	ニ、ふた、ふたつ	two	49 a
桜	オウ、さくら	cherry	桜
徒桜	あだざくら	ephemeral cherry blossoms	49 a
徒	ト　あだ	follower, futility	49 a
刷	サツ、する	print, rub	刷
印刷所	いんさつしょ	printery	49 a
印	イン、しるし	seal, sign, symbol	49 a
所	ショ、ところ	place, situation	49 a

☿	惨	散	傘
49 b	♎	♉	♎

Tragic Scattering of Umbrella Paper.

惨	サン、ザン、みじめ	cruel, miserable	惨
惨劇	さんげき	tragedy	49 b
劇	ゲキ	drama, intense	49 b
散	サン、ちる、ちらす	scatter	散
散髪	さんぱつ	haircut	49 b
髪	ハツ、かみ	hair	49 b
傘	サン、かさ	umbrella, parasol	傘
傘紙	かさがみ	oiled umbrella paper	49 b
紙	シ、かみ	paper	49 b

☿	仕	斬	蚕
49 c	♎	♉	♎

New Ways to Kill Silkworms.

仕	シ、ジ、つかえる	serve, work, do	仕
仕方	しかた	way; method; means	49 c
方	ホウ、かた	side, way, direction	49 c
斬	ザン、サン、セン、きる	beheading; kill	斬
斬新	ざんしん	cutting-edge	49 c
新	シン、あたらしい	new	49 c
蚕	サン、かいこ	silkworm	蚕
養蚕	ようさん	sericulture	49 c
養	ヨウ、やしなう	rear, support	49 c

🔊	伺	使	匹
49 d	♎	♉	♎

An Inquiry into Exploitation of Four Animals.

伺	シ、うかがう	visit, seek, ask, hear	伺
伺い事	うかがいごと	inquiry	49 d
事	ジ、ズ、こと	thing, matter, act	49 d
使	シ、つかう	use, servant, messenger	使
酷使	こくし	expoitation, abuse	49 d
酷	コク	severe, intense, cruel	49 d
匹	ヒツ、ひき	match, cloth, counter	匹
四匹	よんひき	four animals	49 d
四	シ、よ、よつ、よん	four	49 d

🔊	始	姿	姉
49 e	♎	♉	♎

In the Beginning there was the Figure of the Elder Sister.

始	シ、はじめる、はじまる	begin, first	始
始終	しじゅう	throughout	49 e
終	シュウ、おわる、おえる	end, finish	49 e
姿	シ、すがた	form, figure	姿

姿勢	しせい	posture	49 e
勢	セイ、いきおい	power, force	49 e
姉	シ、あね	elder sister	姉
姉妹	しまい	sisters	49 e
妹	マイ、いもうと	younger sister	49 e

8	市	支	施
49 f	♎	♉	♎

This Market has a Branch Office and Facilities.

市	シ、いち	city, market	市
市場	しじょう	market	49 f
場	ジョウ、ば	place	49 f
支	シ、ささえる	branch, support	支
支店	しじ	branch office	49 f
店	テン、みせ	store, premises	49 f
施	シ、セ、ほどこす	perform, charity	施
施設	しせつ	facilities	49 f
設	セツ、もうける	establish, build	49 f

8	止	枝	旨
49 g	♎	♉	♎

Don't Stop the Antlers's Spirits.

止	シ、とまる、とめる	stop	止
中止	ちゅうし	suspension	49 g
中	チュウ、なか	middle, inside, China	49 g
枝	シ、えだ	branch	枝
枝角	えだずの	antlers	49 g
角	カク、かど、つの	horn, angle	49 g
旨	シ、むね	tasty, good, gist	旨
趣旨	しゅし	spirit	49 g
趣	シュ、おもむき	gist, tendency	49 g

	43	44	45	46	47	48	49
a	愚劣	経済	貢献	雇い人	心構え	教唆	二冊
	虞犯	稽古	番犬	虎穴	梗塞	商魂	徒桜
	隅石	跡継ぎ	絹布	股木	控え所	左側	印刷所
b	掘り出す	参詣	賢立つ	回顧	入り江	催促	惨劇
	串刺し	軽少	肩肘	互譲	硬化	挫折	散髪
	岩屋	蛍光	五軒	鼓動	溝泥	封鎖	傘紙
c	熊害	迎え人	経験	悟性	絞め殺す	夫妻	仕方
	長靴	鯨油	打鍵	後盾	耕作	高最	斬新
	桑原	鶏卵	冒険	呉れ手	大綱	色彩	養蚕
d	群衆	隙間	弓弦	成功	乗り降り	採取	伺い事
	薫香	憤激	減少	乞食	鋼鉄	二歳	酷使
	君主	攻撃	幻術	有効	考案	砕氷船	四匹
e	係員	欠乏	無限	厚顔	時刻	裁判	始終
	傾向	清潔	資源	勾引	物腰	国際	姿勢
	兄弟	衣桁	右舷	窓口	合唱	滞在	姉妹
f	契約	兼用	固執	修好	申し込む	坂道	市場
	仁恵	穴埋め	自己	技巧	日頃	罪深い	支店
	休息	剣舞	点呼	大工	貧困	阪神	施設
g	掲載	堅陣	冬枯れ	広告	傷痕	削除	中止
	尊敬	命懸け	車庫	幸福	混乱	搾取	枝角
	提携	嫌悪	故買	慌て者	懇談	埼玉県	趣旨

CHAPTER 8
Weeks 50 – 56

✂	糸	氏	私
50 a	♎	♉	♎

The Silk Family live in a Private Cocoon.

糸	シ、いと	thread	糸
繭糸	けんし	silk thread	50 a
繭	ケン、まゆ	cocoon	50 a
氏	シ、うじ	clan, family, mr	氏
氏名	しめい	full name	50 a
名	メイ、ミョウ、な	name, fame	50 a
私	シ、わたくし	I, private	私
私立	しりつ	private	50 a
立	リツ、リュウ、たつ、たてる	stand, rise, leave	50 a

✂	至	試	諮
50 b	♎	♉	♎

Urgent Tests and Inquiries.

至	シ、いたる	go, reach, peak	至
至急	しきゅう	urgent; pressing	50 b
急	キュウ、いそぐ	emergency, sudden	50 b
試	シ、こころみる、ためす	trial, test	試
試合	しあい	match	50 b
合	ゴウ、ガッ、カッ、あう	meet, join, fit	50 b
諮	シ、はかる	consult, inquire	諮
諮問	しもん	inquiry	50 b
問	モン、とう、とい、とん	ask	50 b

✂	賜	飼	似
50 c	♎	♉	♎

The Gifted Shepherd Resembled his flock.

賜	シ、たまわる	bestow	賜
賜物	たまもの	gift, boon	50 c
物	ブツ、モツ、もの	thing	50 c
飼	シ、かう	rear animals	飼
羊飼い	ひつじかい	shepherd	50 c
羊	ヨウ、ひつじ	sheep	50 c
似	ジ、にる	resemble	似
類似	るいじ	resemblance	50 c
類	ルイ	resemble, variety, sort	50 c

♐	慈	侍	寺
50 d	♎	♉	♎

Affectionate Ladies-In-Waiting worship at the Temple.

慈	ジ、いつくしむ	love, pity, affection	慈
慈善	じぜん	charity	50 d
善	ゼン、よい	good, virtuous	50 d
侍	ジ、さむらい	attend (upon)	侍
侍女	じじょ	lady-in-waiting	50 d
女	ジョ、ニョウ、おんな、め	woman	50 d
寺	ジ、てら	temple	寺
寺院	じいん	buddhist temple	50 d
院	イン	institute	50 d

♐	餌	治	耳
50 e	♎	♉	♎

Fine Food to the mouth is like Healing music to the Ear.

餌	ジ、ニ、えば、えさ、もち	food; bait; prey	餌
好餌	こうじ	tempting offer	50 e
好	コウ、このむ、すく	like, good, fine	50 e
治	ジ、チ、おさめる、おさまる	rule, cure	治
治癒	ちゆ	cure	50 e

癒	ユ		cure, heal, vent	50 e
耳	ジ、みみ		ear	耳
耳鼻科	じびか		otorhinology	50 e
鼻	ビ、はな		nose	50 e
科	カ		course, section	50 e

✂	鹿	叱	執
50 f	♎	♉	♎

Sluggards Scold with admirable Tenacity.

鹿	ロク、か、しか、しし	deer	鹿
馬鹿	ばか	dimwit; sluggard	50 f
馬	バ、うま、ま	horse	50 f
叱	シツ, しかる	scold	叱
叱責	しっせき	reprimand	50 f
責	セキ、せめる	liability, blame	50 f
執	シツ、シュウ、とる	take, grasp, execute	執
執着	しゅうちゃく	attachment; tenacity	50 f
着	チャク、ジャク、きる	arrive, wear	50 f

✂	失	妬	室
50 g	♎	♉	♎

Jealous Loosers were gathering in the Living Room.

失	シツ、うしなう	lose	失
損失	そんしつ	loss	50 g
損	ソン、そこなう、そこねる	loss, spoil, miss	50 g
妬	ト, ねたむ	be jealous	妬
嫉妬	しっと	jealousy	50 g
嫉	シツ、そねむ、ねたむ	jealous; envy	50 g
室	シツ、むろ	room, house	室
居室	きょしつ	living room	50 g
居	キョ、いる	be, reside	50 g

	質	湿	漆
51 a	♎	♉	♎

Quality Moist Lacquer.

質	シツ、シチ、チ	quality, pawn	質
品質	ひんしつ	quality	51 a
品	ヒン、しな	goods, quality	51 a
湿	シツ、しめる、しめす	damp, moist	湿
湿潤	しつじゅん	dampness	51 a
潤	ジュン、うるおう	moisten, enrich	51 a
漆	シツ、うるし	lacquer, varnish	漆
漆塗り	うるしぬり	lacquering	51 a
塗	ト、ぬる	plaster, coat, paint	51 a

	射	捨	写
51 b	♎	♉	♎

Speculation about Abandoned Transcriptions.

射	シャ、いる	shoot	射
射幸	しゃこう	speculation	51 b
幸	コウ、さいわい、しあわせ	happiness, luck	51 b
捨	シャ、すてる	abandon	捨
捨て子	すてご	foundling	51 b
子	シ、ス、こ	child	51 b
写	シャ、うつす、うつる	copy, transcribe	写
描写	びょうしゃ	depiction	51 b
描	ビョウ、えがく	draw, write	51 b

	謝	斜	煮
51 c	♎	♉	♎

Thanking everyone for a Diagonal Boil.

謝	シャ、あやまる	apologize, thank	謝
感謝	かんしゃ	gratitude	51 c
感	カン	feeling	51 c
斜	シャ、ななめ	slanting, diagonal	斜
傾斜	けいしゃ	inclination, slope	51 c
傾	ケイ、かたむく	incline, dedicate	51 c
煮	シャ、にる、にえる	boil, cook	煮
煮立てる	にたてる	bring to boil	51 c
立	リツ、リュウ、たてる	stand, rise, leave	51 c

⚭	酌	蛇	遮
51 d	♎	♉	♎

A Nightcap for the Snakeskin Circuitbreaker.

酌	シャク、くむ	serve wine, ladle	酌
晩酌	ばんしゃく	nightcap'	51 d
晩	バン	evening, late	51 d
蛇	ジャ、ダ、へび	snake, serpent	蛇
蛇革	へびがわ	snakeskin	51 d
革	カク、かわ	leather, reform	51 d
遮	シャ、さえぎる	obstruct, interrupt	遮
遮断器	しゃだんき	circuit-breaker	51 d
断	ダン、たつ、ことわる	cut, decline, warn	51 d
器	キ、うつわ	vessel, utensil, skill	51 d

⚭	殊	若	弱
51 e	♎	♉	♎

In Particular, a Youthful Attraction to Learning is dangerous.

殊	シュ、こと	especially	殊
殊更	ことさら	especially	51 e
更	コウ、さら、ふける	anew, change, again	51 e
若	ジャク、ニャク、わかい	young, if	若

若年	じゃくねん	youth	51 e
年	ネン、とし	year	51 e
弱	ジャク、よわい、よわる	weak	弱
文弱	ぶんじゃく	attraction to learning	51 e
文	ブン、モン、ふみ	writing, text	51 e

| 🔊 | 腫 | 呪 | 寿 |
| 51 f | ♎ | ♉ | ♎ |

Removing the Tumor through Magic increases the Life Span.

腫	シュ、ショウ、はれる、はれ	tumor; swelling	腫
腫瘍	しゅよう	tumor	51 f
瘍	ヨウ かさ	boil; carbuncle	51 f
呪	ジュ、シュ、シュウ、のろい	spell; curse; charm	呪
呪術	じゅじゅつ	magic; incantation	51 f
術	ジュツ	means, technique	51 f
寿	ジュ、ことぶき	long life, congr.	寿
寿命	じゅみょう	life span	51 f
命	メイ、ミョウ、いのち	life, order	51 f

| 🔊 | 就 | 授 | 宗 |
| 51 g | ♎ | ♉ | ♎ |

Finding Employment as a Teacher of Religion.

就	シュウ、ジュ、つく	take up	就
就職	しゅうしょく	finding employmnt	51 g
職	ショク	employment, job	51 g
授	ジュ、さずける、さずかる	confer, teach	授
授業	じゅぎょう	tuition	51 g
業	ギョウ、ゴウ、わざ	profession, deed	51 g
宗	シュウ、ソウ	religion, main	宗
宗教	しゅうきょう	religion	51 g
教	キョウ、おしえる	teach	51 g

○—○	秋	愁	臭
52 a	♎	♉	♎

Autumn's Sad Face Smells like apple pie.

秋	シュウ、あき	autumn	秋
秋分	しゅうぶん	autumn equinox	52 a
分	ブン、フン、ブ、わける	divide	52 a
愁	シュウ、うれえる、うれい	grief, sadness	愁
愁い顔	うれいがお	sad face	52 a
顔	ガン、かお	face	52 a
臭	シュウ、くさい	smell, smack	臭
臭味	くさみ	smell, smack	52 a
味	ミ、あじ、あじわう	taste, relish	52 a

○—○	襲	蹴	舟
52 b	♎	♉	♎

Invasion of Propelled Ferryboats.

襲	シュウ、おそう	attack, inherit	襲
襲来	しゅうらい	invasion	52 b
来	ライ、くる、きたる、きたす	come	52 b
蹴	シュウ、ける	kick	蹴
一蹴	いっしゅう	kick; rejection	52 b
一	イチ、イツ、ひと、ひとつ	one	52 b
舟	シュウ、ふね、ふな	boat	舟
渡し舟	わたしぶね	ferryboat	52 b
渡	ト、わたる、わたす	hand over	52 b

○—○	住	醜	集
52 c	♎	♉	♎

Here Dwells a Scandalous Editor.

住	ジュウ、すむ、すまう	reside, live	住
住居	じゅうきょ	dwelling	52 c
居	キョ、いる	be, reside	52 c
醜	シュウ、みにくい	ugly, shameful	醜
醜聞	しゅうぶん	scandal	52 c
聞	ブン、モン、きく	hear, ask, listen	52 c
集	シュウ、あつまる	gather, collect	集
編集者	へんしゅうしゃ	editor	52 c
編	ヘン、あむ	edit, knit, book	52 c
者	シャ、もの	person	52 c

⊶	充	汁	十
52 d	♎	♉	♎

Enough Gall for a Ten Night's Stay.

充	ジュウ、あてる	full, fill, provide	充
充分	じゅうぶん	enough	52 d
分	ブン、フン、ブ、わける	divide, understand	52 d
汁	ジュウ、しる	juice, soup, liquid	汁
胆汁	たんじゅう	bile; gall	52 d
胆	タン	liver, gall, courage	52 d
十	ジュウ、ジッ、とお、と	ten	十
十泊	じゅうはく	ten night's stay	52 d
泊	ハク、とまる、とめる	stay, lodge	52 d

⊶	柔	従	渋
52 e	♎	♉	♎

Meek Employees were stuck in a Traffic Jam.

柔	ジュウ、ニュウ、やわらか	soft, gentle, weak	柔
柔順	じゅうじゅん	obedient; meek	52 e
順	ジュン	sequence	52 e
従	ジュウ、ショウ、したがう	follow, comply	従

従業員	じゅうぎょういん	employee	52 e
業	ギョウ、ゴウ、わざ	profession, karma	52 e
員	イン	member, official	52 e
渋	ジュウ、しぶ、しぶる	astringent	渋
渋滞	じゅうたい	traffic jam	52 e
滞	タイ、とどこおる	stop, stagnate	52 e

⌒	熟	獣	縦
52 f	♎	♉	♎

Skilled Birds and Wild Animals were resting on Vertical Lines.

熟	ジュク、うれる	ripe, mature, cooked	熟
老熟	ろうじゅく	mature skill, maturity	52 f
老	ロウ、おいる、ふける	old, aged	52 f
獣	ジュウ、けもの	beast	獣
鳥獣	ちょうじゅう	birds and wild animals	52 f
鳥	チョウ、とり	bird	52 f
縦	ジュウ、たて	vertical, selfish	縦
縦線	じゅうせん	vertical line	52 f
線	セン	line	52 f

⌒	瞬	述	春
52 g	♎	♉	♎

Twinkling of the Eyes are Predicated on Spring.

瞬	シュン、またたく	flash, twinkle, blink	瞬
瞬く間	またたくまに	twinkling of an eye	52 g
間	カン、ケン、あいだ、ま	space, gap	52 g
述	ジュツ、のべる	state, relate	述
述語	じゅつご	predicate	52 g
語	ゴ、かたる、かたらう	tell, speak, talk	52 g
春	シュン、はる	spring	春
青春	せいしゅん	youth	52 g

青	セイ、ショウ、あおい	blue, green, young	52 g

☿ 53 a	緒 ♎	初 ♉	暑 ♎

Beginning of First Love in Sultry Weather.

緒	ショ、チョ、お	beginning, cord	緒
一緒	いっしょ	together	53 a
一	イチ、イツ、ひとつ	one	53 a
初	ショ、はじめ、はつ	beginning, first	初
初恋	はつこい	first love	53 a
恋	レン、こう、こい	love, beloved	53 a
暑	ショ、あつい	hot (weather)	暑
蒸し暑い	むしあつい	hot and humid	53 a
蒸	ジョウ、むす、むれる	humid	53 a

☿ 53 b	諸 ♎	勝 ♉	升 ♎

Both Knees Neglected in equal Measure.

諸	ショ、もろ	various, many	諸
諸膝	もろひざ	both knees	53 b
膝	シツ、ひざ	knee; lap	53 b
勝	ショウ、かつ、まさる	win, surpass	勝
怠り勝ち	おこたりがち	neglectful	53 b
怠	タイ、おこたる	be lazy, neglect	53 b
升	ショウ、ます	liquid measure	升
升目	ますめ	measure	53 b
目	モク、ボク、め、ま	eye, ordinal, suffix	53 b

☿ 53 c	招 ♎	宵 ♉	床 ♎

An Inviting Evening Moon shone above the Sickbed.

招	ショウ、まねく	invite, summon	招
招待	しょうたい	invitation	53 c
待	タイ、まつ	wait	53 c
宵	ショウ、よい	evening	宵
宵月	よいずき	evening moon	53 c
月	ゲツ、ガツ、つき	moon	53 c
床	ショウ、とこ、ゆか	bed, floor, alcove	床
病床	びょうしょう	sickbed	53 c
病	ビョウ、ヘイ、やむ、やまい	illness	53 c

☿	昇	沼	松
53 d	♎	♉	♎

Up the Swamp and down the Pine Grove.

昇	ショウ、のぼる	rise, ascend	昇
上昇	じょうしょう	rise, ascend, climb	53 d
上	ジョウ、ショウ、うえ、うわ	up, top, go up	53 d
沼	ショウ、ぬま	swamp, marsh	沼
沼沢	しょうたく	swamp, marsh	53 d
沢	タク、さわ	marsh, much	53 d
松	ショウ、まつ	pine	松
松原	まつばら	pine grove	53 d
原	ゲン、はら	plain, origin	53 d

☿	省	焦	照
53 e	♎	♉	♎

Omit that Charred Illustration.

省	セイ、ショウ、かえりみる	ministry, examine	省
省略	しょうりゃく	abbreviate, omit	53 e
略	リャク	outline	53 e
焦	ショウ、こげる、こがす	scorch, fret	焦
黒焦げ	くろこげ	charring	53 e

黒	コク、くろ、くろい	black	53 e
照	ショウ、てる、てらす	illuminate, shine	照
照明	しょうめい	illustration	53 e
明	メイ、ミョウ、あかり	clear, open, bright	53 e

☿	障	♂	詔
53 f	♎	♉	♎

No Impediment to Robust Imperial Edicts.

障	ショウ、さわる	hinder, block	障
障害	しょうがい	impediment	53 f
害	ガイ	harm, damage	53 f
丈	ジョウ、たけ	length, measure	丈
丈夫	じょうぶ	sturdy, robust	53 f
夫	フ、フウ、おっと	husband, man	53 f
詔	ショウ、みことのり	imperial edict	詔
大詔	たいしょう	imperial edict	53 f
大	ダイ、タイ、おお、おおきい	big	53 f

☿	醸	♂	畳
53 g	♎	♉	♎

Brewing takes place in the Castle's Two-Mat Size dungeon.

醸	ジョウ、かもす	brew, cause	醸
醸造	じょうぞう	brewing	53 g
造	ゾウ、つくる	make, build	53 g
城	ジョウ、しろ	castle	城
城下町	じょうかまち	castle town	53 g
下	カ、ゲ、した、しも	base, under, lower	53 g
町	チョウ、まち	town	53 g
畳	ジョウ、たたむ、たたみ	mat, size, fold	畳
二畳	にじょう	two-mat size	53 g
二	ニ、ふた、ふたつ	two	53 g

♂ 54 a	植 ♎	飾 ♉	拭 ♎

Colonial Decoration was Swept Away.

植	ショク、うえる、うわる	plant	植
植民地	しょくみんち	colony	54 a
民	ミン、たみ	people, populace	54 a
地	チ、ジ	ground, land	54 a
飾	ショク、かざる	decorate	飾
飾り物	かざりもの	decoration	54 a
物	ブツ、モツ、もの	thing	54 a
拭	ショク、シキ、ぬぐう	wipe; mop; swab	拭
払拭	ふっしょく	sweeping away	54 a
払	フツ、はらう	pay, sweep away, rid	54 a

♂ 54 b	殖 ♎	触 ♉	織 ♎

Developing Tactile Ridged Fabric.

殖	ショク、ふえる、ふやす	increase, enrich	殖
拓殖	たくしょく	colonize, develop	54 b
拓	タク	reclaim, clear, rub	54 b
触	ショク、ふれる、さわる	feel, touch, contact	触
接触	せっしょく	contact	54 b
接	セツ、つぐ	contact, join	54 b
織	ショク、シキ、おる	weave	織
畝織	うねおり	ridged fabric	54 b
畝	せ、うね	ridge, measure	54 b

♂ 54 c	伸 ♎	尻 ♉	辱 ♎

Extending Excessiveness to a Disgraceful degree.

伸	シン、のびる、のばす	stretch, extend	伸
伸縮	しんしゅく	elasticity	54 c
縮	シュク、ちぢむ、ちぢまる	shrink, reduce	54 c
尻	コウ、しり	buttocks; hips; butt	尻
尻癖	しりくせ	incontinence	54 c
癖	ヘキ、くせ	habit, kink	54 c
辱	ジョク、はずかしめる	insult, humiliate	辱
恥辱	ちじょく	disgrace	54 c
恥	チ、はじる、はじらう	shame, ashamed	54 c

☿	慎	寝	唇
54 d	♎	♉	♎

Discretely Sleepy Lips.

慎	シン、つつしむ	be discreet	慎
慎み深い	つつしみぶかい	discreet	54 d
深	シン、ふかい	deep, deepen	54 d
寝	シン、ねる、ねかす	sleep, lie down	寝
寝具	しんぐ	bedding	54 d
具	グ	equip, means	54 d
唇	シン、くちびる	lip(s)	唇
口唇	こうしん	lips	54 d
口	コウ、ク、くち	mouth, opening	54 d

☿	浸	森	振
54 e	♎	♉	♎

Immersive Solemn Behaviour.

浸	シン、ひたす、ひたる	soak, immerse	浸
浸水	しんすい	inundation	54 e
水	スイ、みず	water	54 e
森	シン、もり	woods	森
森厳	しんげん な	solemn	54 e

厳	ゲン、ゴン、おごそか	severe, strict, solemn	54 e
振	シン、ふる、ふるう	wave, swing, air	振
振舞い	ふるまい	behaviour	54 e
舞	ブ、まう、まい	dance, flit	54 e

☿	臣	親	薪
54 f	♎	♉	♎

Minister for Friendly Woodchopping.

臣	シン、ジン	retainer, subject	臣
大臣	だいじん	minister	54 f
大	ダイ、タイ、おおきい	big	54 f
親	シン、おや、したしむ	intimate, parent	親
親善	しんぜん	friendship	54 f
善	ゼン、よい	good, virtuous	54 f
薪	シン、たきぎ	firewood	薪
薪割り	まきわり	woodchopping	54 f
割	カツ、わる、わり、われる	divide, rate	54 f

☿	診	身	辛
54 g	♎	♉	♎

Diagnosis of Ranking Hardship.

診	シン、みる	diagnose, examine	診
診断	しんだん	diagnosis	54 g
断	ダン、たつ、ことわる	cut, decline, warn, judge	54 g
身	シン、み	body	身
身分	みぶん	status	54 g
分	ブン、フン、ブ、わける	divide, understand	54 g
辛	シン、からい	sharp, bitter	辛
辛苦	しんく	hardship	54 g
苦	ク、くるしむ、にがい	painful, bitter	54 g

☿	尋	針	刃
55 a	♎	♉	♎

Under Questioning, the Needle and Blade are effective.

尋	ジン、たずねる	ask, inquire, a fathom	尋
尋問	じんもん	questioning	55 a
問	モン、とう、とい、とん	ask	55 a
針	シン、はり	needle	針
磁針	じしん	magnetic needle	55 a
磁	ジ	magnet, porcelain	55 a
刃	ジン、は	blade, sword	刃
刃物	はもの	bladed object	55 a
物	ブツ、モツ、もの	thing	55 a

☿	甚	尽	須
55 b	♎	♉	♎

Immensely Exhaustive Necessary actions.

甚	ジン、はなはだ	great(ly)	甚
甚大	じんだい な	immense	55 b
大	ダイ、タイ、おおきい	big	55 b
尽	ジン、つくす、つきる	use up, exhaust	尽
焼き尽くす	やきつくす	burn up, consume	55 b
焼	ショウ、やく、やける	burn, roast	55 b
須	ス、あごひげ	by all means	須
必須	ひっす	necessary	55 b
必	ヒツ、かならず	necessarily	55 b

☿	酢	図	吹
55 c	♎	♉	♎

Sour Undirected Exhalations.

酢	サク、す	vinegar, sour	酢
酢の物	すのもの	pickles	55 c
物	ブツ、モツ、もの	thing	55 c
図	ズ、ト、はかる	map; drawing; plan	図
指図	さしず	directions	55 c
指	シ、ゆび、さす	finger, point	55 c
吹	スイ、ふく	blow, breathe out	吹
吹き倒す	ふきたおす	blow down	55 c
倒	トウ、たおれる	fall, topple, invert	55 c

☿	衰	粋	炊
55 d	♎	♉	♎

Decline of Stylish Cooking.

衰	スイ、おとろえる	become weak, wither	衰
衰退	すいたい	decline, degeneration	55 d
退	タイ、しりぞく	retreat, withdraw	55 d
粋	スイ	pure, essence, style	粋
粋人	すいじん	man of taste	55 d
人	ジン、ニン、ひと	person	55 d
炊	スイ、たく	cook, boil	炊
炊事	すいじ	cooking	55 d
事	ジ、ズ、こと	thing, matter, act	55 d

☿	酔	遂	数
55 e	♎	♉	♎

That Drunk Made an Attempt at Mathematics.

酔	スイ、よう	drunk, dizzy	酔
酔払い	よっぱらい	drunkard	55 e
払	フツ、はらう	pay, sweep away	55 e
遂	スイ、とげる	attain, finally	遂
未遂	みすいの	attempted	55 e

未	ミ	immature, not yet	55 e
数	スウ、ス、かず、かぞえる	number, count	数
数学	すうがく	mathematics	55 e
学	ガク、まなぶ	study	55 e

☿	澄	据	裾
55 f	♎	♉	♎

Clean Installations near the Foothills.

澄	チョウ、すむ、すます	clear, settle	澄
清澄	せいちょうな	clear	55 f
清	セイ、ショウ、きよい	pure, clean	55 f
据	すえる、すわる	set, place, sit	据
据え付け	すえつけ	installation	55 f
付	フ、つける、つく	attach, apply	55 f
裾	キョ、すそ	foot of mountain	裾
裾野	すその	foothills	55 f
野	ヤ、の	moor, wild	55 f

☿	世	凄	姓
55 g	♎	♉	♎

In the Fleeting World of Uncanny Surnames.

世	セイ、セ、よ	world, society, age	世
浮き世	うきよ	fleeting world	55 g
浮	フ、うく、うかれる	float, fleeting. gay	55 g
凄	サイ、セイ、すさまじい	uncanny; horrible	凄
凄惨	せいさん	ghostliness	55 g
惨	サン、ザン、みじめ	cruel, miserable	55 g
姓	セイ、ショウ	surname	姓
姓名	せいめい	surname	55 g
名	メイ、ミョウ、な	name, fame	55 g

☿	晴	精	整
56 a	♎	♉	♎

The Stylish Fairy had to pay Maintenance.

晴	セイ、はれる	clear, bright	晴
晴れ姿	はれすがた	app. in one's finest clothes	56 a
姿	シ、すがた	form, figure	56 a
精	セイ、ショウ	spirit, vitality, refine	精
妖精	ようせい	fairy	56 a
妖	ヨウ、あやしい	attractive	56 a
整	セイ、ととのえる	arrange	整
整備	せいび	maintenance	56 a
備	ビ、そなえる	equip, prepare	56 a

☿	声	誓	逝
56 b	♎	♉	♎

That Jeering Pledge hastened his Sudden Death.

声	セイ、ショウ、こえ、こわ	voice	声
罵声	ばせい	jeers	56 b
罵	バ、ののしる	abuse; insult	56 b
誓	セイ、ちかう	pledge, vow, oath	誓
誓約	せいやく	pledge	56 b
約	ヤク	promise	56 b
逝	セイ、ゆく	die, pass on, death	逝
急逝	きゅうせい	sudden death	56 b
急	キュウ、いそぐ	emergency, sudden	56 b

☿	醒	惜	戚
56 c	♎	♉	♎

Disillusioned by Loathsome Relatives.

醒	セイ、さます	be dillusioned	醒
覚醒剤	かくせいざい	stimulant drugs	56 c
覚	カク、おぼえる、さます	remember, learn	56 c
剤	ザイ	medicine, drug	56 c
惜	セキ、おしい、おしむ	regret, be loath to	惜
惜し気	おしげ	regret	56 c
気	キ、ケ	spirit	56 c
戚	セキ、いたむ、うれえる	grieve	戚
親戚	しんせき	relatives	56 c
親	シン、おや、したしむ	intimate, parent	56 c

☿	積	昔	脊
56 d	♎	♉	♎

Accumulating Past and Present on the Spinal Cord.

積	セキ、つむ、つもる	product, pile	積
堆積	たいせき	accumulation	56 d
堆	タイ、ツイ、うずたかい	piled high	56 d
昔	セキ、シャク、むかし	olden times, past	昔
今昔	こんじゃく	past and present	56 d
今	コン、キン、いま	now	56 d
脊	セキ、せ、せい	stature; height	脊
脊髄	せきずい	spinal cord	56 d
髄	ズイ	marrow	56 d

☿	説	赤	節
56 e	♎	♉	♎

Persuaded by a Scarlet Hip Joint.

説	セツ、ゼイ、とく	preach, explain	説
説得	せっとく	persuasion	56 e
得	トク、える、うる	gain, potential	56 e
赤	セキ、シャク、あかい	red	赤

赤面	せきめん	blush	56 e
面	メン、おも、おもて	face, aspect, mask	56 e
節	セツ、セチ、ふし	section, joint, period	節
股関節	こかんせつ	hip joint	56 e
股	コ、また、もも	thigh; crotch; yarn	56 e
関	カン、せき	connection	56 e

☿	占	千	雪
56 f	♎	♉	♎

Divining Thousands of words in woolly Snowflakes.

占	セン、しめる、うらなう	divine, occupy	占
占い者	うらないしゃ	diviner	56 f
者	シャ、もの	person	56 f
千	セン、ち	thousand	千
千言	んせんげん	lots of words	56 f
言	ゲン、ゴン、いう、こと	word, say, speak	56 f
雪	セツ、ゆき	snow	雪
綿雪	わたゆき	large snowflakes	56 f
綿	メン、わた	cotton, cotton wool	56 f

☿	専	扇	戦
56 g	♎	♉	♎

Exclusively for Fans of Major Wars.

専	セン、もっぱら	exclusive, sole	専
専門	せんもん	speciality	56 g
門	モン、かど	gate, door	56 g
扇	セン、おうぎ	fan	扇
扇子	せんす	(folding) fan	56 g
子	シ、ス、こ	child	56 g
戦	セン、いくさ、たたかう	fight, war	戦
大戦	たいせん	major war	56 g
大	ダイ、タイ、おおいに	big	56 g

	50	51	52	53	54	55	56
a	繭糸	品質	秋分	一緒	植民地	尋問	晴れ姿
	氏名	湿潤	愁い顔	初恋	飾り物	磁針	妖精
	私立	漆塗り	臭味	蒸し暑い	払拭	刃物	整備
b	至急	射幸	襲来	諸膝	拓殖	甚大	罵声
	試合	捨て子	一蹴	怠り勝ち	接触	焼き尽くす	誓約
	諮問	描写	渡し舟	升目	畝織	必須	急逝
c	賜物	感謝	住居	招待	伸縮	酢の物	覚醒剤
	羊飼い	傾斜	醜聞	宵月	尻癖	指図	惜し気
	類似	煮立てる	編集者	病床	恥辱	吹き倒す	親戚
d	慈善	晩酌	充分	上昇	慎み深い	衰退	堆積
	侍女	蛇革	胆汁	沼沢	寝具	粋人	今昔
	寺院	遮断器	十泊	松原	口唇	炊事	脊髄
e	好餌	殊更	柔順	省略	浸水	酔払い	説得
	治癒	若年	従業員	黒焦げ	森厳	未遂	赤面
	耳鼻科	文弱	渋滞	照明	振舞い	数学	股関節
f	馬鹿	腫瘍	老熟	障害	大臣	清澄	占い者
	叱責	呪術	鳥獣	丈夫	親善	据え付け	千言
	執着	寿命	縦線	大詔	薪割り	裾野	綿雪
g	損失	就職	瞬く間	醸造	診断	浮き世	専門
	嫉妬	授業	述語	城下町	身分	凄惨	扇子
	居室	宗教	青春	二畳	辛苦	姓名	大戦

CHAPTER 9
Weeks 57 – 63

♀	潜	浅	染
57 a	♎	♉	♎

Dangerous Diving in Shallow pools of Dye.

潜	セン、ひそむ、もぐる	dive, lurk, hide	潜
潜水	せんすい	diving	57 a
水	スイ、みず	water	57 a
浅	セン、あさい	shallow, light	浅
浅薄	せんぱく	shallowness	57 a
薄	ハク、うすい、うすめる	thin, weak	57 a
染	セン、そめる、しみる	dye, soak	染
色染め	いろぞめ	dyeing	57 a
色	ショク、シキ、いろ	colour	57 a

♀	薦	煎	羨
57 b	♎	♉	♎

Recommending Rice Crackers without Resentment.

薦	セン、すすめる	recommend, mat	薦
推薦	すいせん	recommendation	57 b
推	スイ、おす	infer, push ahead	57 b
煎	セン、いる	parched	煎
煎餅	せんべい	rice crackers	57 b
餅	ヘイ、もち	mochi rice cake	57 b
羨	セン、うらやむ	envious	羨
羨望	せんぼう	envy	57 b
望	ボウ、モウ、のぞむ	wish, hope, gaze	57 b

♀	鮮	詮	銭
57 c	♎	♉	♎

Vivid Discussions in the Public Bath.

鮮	セン、あざやか	fresh, vivid, clear	鮮
鮮明	せんめい な	clear, vivid	57 c
明	メイ、ミョウ、あかるい	clear, open, bright	57 c
詮	セン、そなわる	discussion; selection	詮
詮索	せんさく	inquiry into	57 c
索	サク	rope, search	57 c
銭	セン、ぜに	sen, coin, money	銭
銭湯	せんとう	public bath	57 c
湯	トウ、ゆ	hot water	57 c

✿	狙	繕	疎
57 d	♎	♉	♎

Instead of Sniping, let's try to mend feelings of Alienation.

狙	ソ、ショ、ねらう、ねらい	aim at; sight; stalk	狙
狙撃	そげき	sniping	57 d
撃	ゲキ、うつ	strike, attack, fire	57 d
繕	ゼン、つくろう	repair, mend	繕
修繕	しゅうぜん	repairs	57 d
修	シュウ、シュ、おさめる	practice, master	57 d
疎	ソ、うとい、うとむ	distant, shun, coarse	疎
疎外	そがい	alienation	57 d
外	ガイ、そと、ほか、はずす	outside, other, undo	57 d

✿	組	阻	遡
57 e	♎	♉	♎

United in a Spirit of Dejection, we are Sailing Against the Current.

組	ソ、くむ、くみ	group, assemble	組
組合	くみあい	union	57 e
合	ゴウ、ガッ、カッ、あう	meet, join, fit	57 e
阻	ソ、はばむ	obstruct, hinder	阻
阻喪	そそう	dejection	57 e

喪	ソウ、も	mourn, loss, death	57 e
遡	ソ、さかのぼる	go upstream	遡
遡行	そこう	sailing ag. the current	57 e
行	コウ、ギョウ、いく	go, conduct, column	57 e

⚥	創	双	倉
57 f	♎	♉	♎

Creating Pairs of Warehouse Goods.

創	ソウ	start, wound	創
創造	そうぞう	creation	57 f
造	ゾウ、つくる	make, build	57 f
双	ソウ、ふた	pair, both	双
双方	そうほう	both sides	57 f
方	ホウ、かた	side, way, square, direction	57 f
倉	ソウ、くら	warehouse, sudden	倉
倉荷	くらに	warehouse goods	57 f
荷	カ、に	load, burden	57 f

⚥	想	爽	奏
57 g	♎	♉	♎

A Delusional but Thrilling Play.

想	ソウ、ソ	idea, thought	想
妄想	もうそう	delusion	57 g
妄	モウ、ボウ	irrational, rash	57 g
爽	ソウ、さわやか	refreshing	爽
爽快	そうかい	thrilling	57 g
快	カイ、こころよい	pleasant, cheerful	57 g
奏	ソウ、かなでる	play, present, report	奏
伴奏	ばんそう	accompaniment (music)	57 g
伴	ハン、バン、ともなう	accompany	57 g

☉	挿	早	掃
58 a	♎	♉	♎

Illustrating Fast and exciting Vacuum Cleaners.

挿	ソウ、さす	insert	挿
挿絵	さしえ	(book) illustration	58 a
絵	カイ、エ	picture	58 a
早	ソウ、サッ、はやまる	early, fast, prompt	早
素早い	すばやい	fast, quick, nimble	58 a
素	ソ、ス	element, base, bare	58 a
掃	ソウ、はく	sweep	掃
掃除機	そうじき	vacuum cleaner	58 a
除	ジョ、ジ、のぞく	exlude, remove	58 a
機	キ、はた	loom, device, occasion	58 a

☉	紛	痩	巣
58 b	♎	♉	♎

Finally the Querulous and Skinny offspring is Leaving the Nest.

紛	フン、まぎれる、まぎらす	confusion, stray	紛
紛争	ふんそう	dispute	58 b
争	ソウ、あらそう	conflict, vie	58 b
痩	ソウ、やせる	get thin	痩
痩身	そうしん	a lean figure	58 b
身	シン、み	body	58 b
巣	ソウ、す	nest	巣
巣立つ	すだつ	leave nest	58 b
立	リツ、リュウ、たつ	stand, rise, leave	58 b

☉	装	草	藻
58 c	♎	♉	♎

Disguised in Green Grass and Seaweed.

装	ソウ、ショウ、よそおう	wear, clothing, gear	装
変装	へんそう	disguise	58 c
変	ヘン、かわる、かえる	change, strange	58 c
草	ソウ、くさ	grass	草
青草	あおくさ	green grass	58 c
青	セイ、ショウ、あおい	blue, green, young	58 c
藻	ソウ、も	waterweed, seaweed	藻
海藻	かいそう	seaweed	58 c
海	カイ、うみ	sea	58 c

| ☿ | 騒 | 増 | 霜 |
| 58 d | ♎ | ♉ | ♎ |

Chaotic Build Up of Frost Damage.

騒	ソウ、さわぐ	noise, disturbance	騒
大騒ぎ	おうさわぎ	uproar, chaos	58 d
大	ダイ、タイ、おおきい	big	58 d
増	ゾウ、ま-す、ふえる	increase, build up	増
増大	ぞうだい	increase	58 d
大	ダイ、タイ、おおきい	big	58 d
霜	ソウ、しも	frost	霜
霜害	そうがい	frost damage	58 d
害	ガイ	harm, damage	58 d

| ☿ | 貯 | 贈 | 憎 |
| 58 e | ♎ | ♉ | ♎ |

Preservation of Bribes and Malice.

貯	チョ	store, save	貯
貯蔵	ちょぞう	storage; preservation	58 e
蔵	ゾウ、くら	storehouse, harbor	58 e
贈	ゾウ、ソウ、おくる	present, give	贈
贈賄	ぞうわい	bribery	58 e

賄	ワイ、まかなう	bribe, provide, board	58 e
憎	ゾウ、にくむ、にくい	hate(ful)	憎
憎悪	ぞうお	malice, hatred	58 e
悪	アク、オ、わるい	bad, hate	58 e

☼	捉	足	束
58 f	♎	♉	♎

Capture a Satisfactory Moment.

捉	ソク、とらえる	catch; capture	捉
捕捉	ほそく	capture; seizure	58 f
捕	ホ、とらえる、とる	seize, capture	58 f
足	ソク、あし、たりる	foot, sufficient	足
満足	まんぞく	satisfaction	58 f
満	マン、みちる、みたす	full, fill	58 f
束	ソク、たば	bundle, manage	束
束の間	つかのま	moment	58 f
間	カン、ケン、あいだ、ま	space, gap	58 f

☼	続	他	孫
58 g	♎	♉	♎

A Series of Strange Descendants.

続	ゾク、つづく、つづける	continue, series	続
手続き	てつづき	procedure	58 g
手	シュ、て、た	hand	58 g
他	タ	other	他
他人	たにん	stranger	58 g
人	ジン、ニン、ひと	person	58 g
孫	ソン、まご	descendants	孫
子孫	しそん	descendants	58 g
子	シ、ス、こ	child	58 g

☿ 59 a	多 ♎	唾 ♉	対 ♎

Many instances of Despicable Suitability.

多	タ、おおい	many	多
多忙な	たぼうな	very busy	59 a
忙	ボウ、いそがしい	busy	59 a
唾	ダ、タ、つばき	saliva; sputum	唾
唾棄	だき	despicable	59 a
棄	キ	abandon, renounce	59 a
対	タイ、ツイ	against, vis-a-vis, versus	対
対応	たいおう	suitability; compatibility	59 a
応	オウ	respond, react	59 a

☿ 59 b	戴 ♎	替 ♉	耐 ♎

Elderly Money Changers have Patience.

戴	タイ、いただく	receive	戴
戴白	たいはく	old people	59 b
白	ハク、ビャク、しろい	white	59 b
替	タイ、かえる、かわる	exchange, swap	替
両替え	りょうがえ	money changing	59 b
両	リョウ	both, pair, coin	59 b
耐	タイ、たえる	endure, bear	耐
忍耐	にんたい	patience	59 b
忍	ニン、しのぶ、しのばせる	endure, stealth	59 b

☿ 59 c	奪 ♎	濁 ♉	貸 ♎

Recovering a Dirty Loan.

奪	ダツ、うばう	snatch, captivate	奪
奪回	だっかい	recovery	59 c
回	カイ、エ、まわる、まわす	turn, rotate	59 c
濁	ダク、にごる、にごす	impure, voiced	濁
濁音	だくおん	voiced sound	59 c
音	オン、イン、おと、ね	sound	59 c
貸	タイ、かす	lend, loan	貸
貸し金	かしきん	loan	59 c
金	キン、コン、かね、かな	gold, money	59 c

♂	誰	嘆	担
59 d	♎	♉	♎

Somebody Sighed after taking Responsibility.

誰	スイ、だれ	who; somebody	誰
誰某	だれそれ	a certain someone	59 d
某	ボウ、それがし、なにがし	a certain-, some-	59 d
嘆	タン、なげく	lament, admire	嘆
嘆息	たんそく	sigh	59 d
息	ソク、いき	breath, rest, child	59 d
担	タン、かつぐ、になう	carry, bear	担
担当	たんとう	responsibility	59 d
当	トウ、あたる、あてる	apply, hit	59 d

♂	綻	短	淡
59 e	♎	♉	♎

Failures, Shortcomings and Indifference.

綻	タン ほころびる	be rent; ripped; unravel	綻
破綻	はたん	failure	59 e
破	ハ、やぶる、やぶれる	break, tear	59 e
短	タン、みじかい	short	短
短所	たんしょ	shortcoming	59 e

所	ショ、ところ	place, situation	59 e
淡	タン、あわい	pale, light, faint	淡
冷淡	れいたん	coolness; indifference	59 e
冷	レイ、つめたい、ひえる	freeze, cold	59 e

♂	暖	男	壇
59 f	♎	♉	♎

Hot Actors in Flower Beds.

暖	ダン、あたたかい、あたたまる	warm	暖
暖炉	だんろ	fireplace, stove	59 f
炉	ロ	furnace	59 f
男	ダン、ナン、おとこ	man, male	男
男優	だんゆう	actor	59 f
優	ユウ、やさしい、すぐれる	gentle, actor	59 f
壇	ダン、タン	stage, rostrum	壇
花壇	かだん	flower bed	59 f
花	カ、はな	flower, blossom	59 f

♂	知	値	池
59 g	♎	♉	♎

Acquainted with the Price of the Reservoir.

知	チ、しる	know	知
知合い	しりあい	acquaintance	59 g
合	ゴウ、ガッ、カッ、あう	meet, join, fit	59 g
値	チ、ね、あたい	price, value	値
値段	ねだん	price	59 g
段	ダン	step, grade	59 g
池	チ、いけ	pond, lake	池
用水池	ようすいち	reservoir	59 g
用	ヨウ、もちいる	use	59 g
水	スイ、みず	water	59 g

☿	遅	致	築
60 a	♎	♉	♎

Sluggish Kidnappers were found in the Building.

遅	チ、おくれる、おそい	tardy, slow, late	遅
遅咲き	おそざき	late blooming	60 a
咲	さく	blossom	60 a
致	チ、いたす	do, send, cause	致
拉致	らち	kidnapping	60 a
拉	ラツ、ラ、らっする	Latin; kidnap; crush	60 a
築	チク、きずく	build	築
建築	けんちく	building	60 a
建	ケン、コン、たてる	build, erect	60 a

☿	仲	沖	竹
60 b	♎	♉	♎

The Agency's logo was an Okinawan Bamboo Bundle.

仲	チュウ、なか	relationship	仲
仲介	ちゅうかい	agency	60 b
介	カイ	mediate, shell	60 b
沖	チュウ、おき	open sea, soar	沖
沖縄	おきなわ	Okinawa	60 b
縄	ジョウ、なわ	rope, cord	60 b
竹	チク、たけ	bamboo	竹
竹束	たけたば	bamboo bundle	60 b
束	ソク、たば	bundle, manage	60 b

☿	著	注	昼
60 c	♎	♉	♎

The Author Poured a stiff drink in Broad Daylight.

著	チョ、あらわす、いちじるしい	write book	著
著者	ちょしゃ	author	60 c
者	シャ、もの	person	60 c
注	チュウ、そそぐ	pour, note	注
注射	ちゅうしゃ	injection	60 c
射	シャ、いる	shoot	60 c
昼	チュウ、ひる	daytime, noon	昼
真昼	まひる	broad daylight	60 c
真	シン、ま	true	60 c

☿	彫	徴	懲
60 d	♎	♉	♎

Carving out Characteristic Castigation.

彫	チョウ、ほる	carve, sculpture	彫
彫刻	ちょうこく	sculpture	60 d
刻	コク、きざむ	chop, mince, engrave	60 d
徴	チョウ、しるし	sign, summon, levy	徴
特徴	とくちょう	characteristic	60 d
特	トク	special	60 d
懲	チョウ、こりる、こらす	chastise, learn	懲
懲罰	ちょうばつ	punishment	60 d
罰	バツ、バチ	penalty, punishment	60 d

☿	潮	朝	挑
60 e	♎	♉	♎

With the Tide came Imperial Challenges.

潮	チョウ、しお	tide, seawater	潮
潮流	ちょうりゅう	tide, current	60 e
流	リュウ、ル、ながれる	flow, stream	60 e
朝	チョウ、あさ	court, morning	朝
朝廷	ちょうてい	imperial court	60 e

廷	テイ	court, gov. office	60 e
挑	チョウ、いどむ	challenge, defy	挑
挑戦	ちょうせん	challenge	60 e
戦	セン、いくさ、たたかう	fight, war	60 e

☿	眺	超	聴
60 f	♎	♉	♎

Looking through Superman's Stethoscope.

眺	チョウ、ながめる	gaze, look	眺
眺望	ちょうぼう	prospect; view	60 f
望	ボウ、モウ、のぞむ	wish, hope, gaze	60 f
超	チョウ、こえる、こす	exceed, super-	超
超人	ちょうじん	superman	60 f
人	ジン、ニン、ひと	person	60 f
聴	チョウ、きく	listen (carefully)	聴
聴心器	ちょうしんき	stethoscope	60 f
心	シン、こころ	heart, feelings	60 f
器	キ、うつわ	vessel, utensil, skill	60 f

☿	沈	跳	捗
60 g	♎	♉	♎

Silent Springs Make Progress.

沈	チン、しずむ、しずめる	sink	沈
沈黙	ちんもく	silence	60 g
黙	モク、だまる	be silent	60 g
跳	チョウ、はねる、とぶ	spring, jump, leap	跳
跳ね返る	はなかえる	rebound	60 g
返	ヘン、かえす、かえる	return	60 g
捗	チョク、ホ、はかどる	make progress	捗
進捗	しんちょく	progress	60 g
進	シン、すすむ、すすめる	advance	60 g

	追	津	椎
61 a	♎	♉	♎

Banish those Billowing Backbones.

追	ツイ、おう	chase, pursue	追
追放	ついほう	banishment	61 a
放	ホウ、はなす、はなつ	release, emit	61 a
津	シン、つ	harbour, crossing	津
津波	つなみ	tsunami	61 a
波	ハ、なみ	wave	61 a
椎	ツイ、しい	oak; mallet	椎
椎骨	ついこつ	vertebrae	61 a
骨	コツ、ほね	bone, frame	61 a

	爪	漬	潰
61 b	♎	♉	♎

Clawing and Picking at Carbuncles.

爪	ソウ、つめ	claw	爪
生爪	なまづめ	fingernail	61 b
生	セイ、ショウ、いきる、うまれる	life, birth	61 b
漬	つける、つかる	pickle, soak	漬
漬物	つけもの	pickles	61 b
物	ブツ、モツ、もの	thing	61 b
潰	カイ、エ、つぶす、つぶ．れる	crush; break	潰
潰瘍	かいよう	ulcer	61 b
瘍	ヨウ、かさ	carbuncle	61 b

	鶴	低	釣
61 c	♎	♉	♎

Craning the neck for a Low-lying Fishing Spot.

鶴	カク、つる	crane; stork	鶴
鶴首	かくしゅ	looking forward to	61 c
首	シュ、くび	head, neck, chief	61 c
低	テイ、ひくい、ひくめる	low	低
低落	ていらく	decline	61 c
落	ラク、おちる、おとす	fall, drop	61 c
釣	チョウ、つる	fish, lure, change	釣
釣り場	つりば	fishing spot	61 c
場	ジョウ、ば	place	61 c

☿	程	堤	締
61 d	♎	♉	♎

To a large Degree, we are Banking on financial Tightening.

程	テイ、ほど	degree, extent	程
程度	ていど	degree, extent	61 d
度	ド、ト、タク、たび	degree, times	61 d
堤	テイ、つつみ	embankment	堤
堤防	ていぼう	levee, dyke	61 d
防	ボウ、ふせぐ	prevent, defend	61 d
締	テイ、しまる、しめる	bind, tighten, close	締
引締め	ひきしめ	tightening	61 d
引	イン、ひく、ひける	pull, draw	61 d

☿	摘	諦	敵
61 e	♎	♉	♎

Exposing a Clear Picture of Hostility.

摘	テキ、つむ	pluck, pick, extract	摘
摘発	てきはつ	exposure	61 e
発	ハツ、ホツ	discharge, start, leave	61 e
諦	テイ、あきらめる	abandon; give up	諦
諦観	ていかん	clear vision	61 e

観	カン	watch, observe	61 e
敵	テキ、かたき	match, enemy	敵
敵意	てきい	hostility	61 e
意	イ	mind, thought, will	61 e

☿	滴	溺	填
61 f	♎	♉	♎

Dripping Water in Blind Love doesn't Compensate for real tears.

滴	テキ、しずく、したたる	drop, drip	滴
水滴	すいてき	water drop	61 f
水	スイ、みず	water	61 f
溺	デキ, おぼれる	drown	溺
溺愛	できあい	blind love	61 f
愛	アイ	love	61 f
填	テン、いただき	fill in	填
補填	ほてん	compensate for	61 f
補	ホ、おぎなう	make good, stopgap	61 f

☿	添	貼	転
61 g	♎	♉	♎

Accompanying a Pasty Driver.

添	テン、そえる、そう	accompany, add	添
添乗	てんじょう	accompanying	61 g
乗	ジョウ、のる、のせる	ride, mount, load	61 g
貼	チョウ、テン、はる	stick; paste; apply	貼
貼付	ちょうふ	pasting; paste	61 g
付	フ、つける、つく	attach, apply	61 g
転	テン、ころがる	rotate, roll, tumble	転
運転	うんてん	driving	61 g
運	ウン、はこぶ	transport, luck, move	61 g

☿	殿	登	吐
62 a	♎	♉	♎

Lords of Mountaineering voiced their displeasure.

殿	デン、テン、との、どの	palace, lord, mr	殿
宮殿	きゅうでん	palace	62 a
宮	キュウ、グウ、ク、みや	palace, shrine, prince	62 a
登	トウ、ト、のぼる	climb	登
登山	とざん	mountaineering	62 a
山	サン、やま	mountain	62 a
吐	ト、はく	disgorge, vomit	吐
音吐	おんと	voice	62 a
音	オン、イン、おと、ね	sound	62 a

☿	賭	都	努
62 b	♎	♉	♎

In the Gambling Hall of Capital Consolation Prizes are not awarded.

賭	ト、かける、かけ	gamble; wager; bet	賭
賭場	とば	gambling hall	62 b
場	ジョウ、ば	place	62 b
都	ト、ツ、みやこ	capital, metropolis	都
首都	しゅと	capital	62 b
首	シュ、くび	head, neck, chief	62 b
努	ド、つとめる	endeavour, try	努
努力賞	どりょくしょう	consolation prize	62 b
力	リョク、リキ、ちから	strength, effort	62 b
賞	ショウ	prize, praise	62 b

☿	凍	怒	刀
62 c	♎	♉	♎

With a Chilling Cry the Sword was drawn.

凍	トウ、こおる、こごえる	freeze	凍
凍結	とうけつ	freezing	62 c
結	ケツ、むすぶ、ゆわえる	bind, join, end	62 c
怒	ド、いかる、おこる	anger, rage	怒
怒鳴る	どなる	shout, bawl	62 c
鳴	メイ、なく、なる、ならす	cry, chirp, bark	62 c
刀	トウ、かたな	sword	刀
刀刃	とうじん	sword blade	62 c
刃	ジン、は	blade, sword	62 c

☗	唐	島	悼
62 d	♎	♉	♎

Chinese Peninsula in Mourning.

唐	トウ、から	(T'ang) China	唐
唐本	とうほん	Chinese book	62 d
本	ホン、もと	root, true, book, this	62 d
島	トウ、しま	island	島
半島	はんとう	peninsula	62 d
半	ハン、なかば	half, middle	62 d
悼	トウ、いたむ	grieve, mourn	悼
哀悼	あいとう	mourning	62 d
哀	アイ、あわれ、あわれむ	sorrow, pity	62 d

☗	等	桃	棟
62 e	♎	♉	♎

First Class Peaches in the Ward.

等	トウ、ひとしい	class, equal	等
一等	いっとう	first class	62 e
一	イチ、イツ、ひと、ひとつ	one	62 e
桃	トウ、もも	peach	桃
桃色	ももいろ	pink	62 e

色	ショク、シキ、いろ	colour, sensuality	62 e
棟	トウ、むね、むな	ridgepole, building	棟
病棟	びょうとう	ward	62 e
病	ビョウ、ヘイ、やむ	illness	62 e

♁	筒	豆	答
62 f	♎	♉	♎

Cylindrical Tofu Solutions.

筒	トウ、つつ	tube, cylinder	筒
筒形	つつがた	cylindrical	62 f
形	ケイ、ギョウ、かた、かたち	shape, pattern	62 f
豆	トウ、ズ、まめ	beans, miniature	豆
豆腐	とうふ	tofu	62 f
腐	フ、くさる、くされる	rot, decay, bad	62 f
答	トウ、こたえる、こたえ	answer	答
解答	かいとう	solution	62 f
解	カイ、ゲ、とく、とかす	explain, solve	62 f

♁	透	踏	逃
62 g	♎	♉	♎

Clearly Stepping into Escape Routes.

透	トウ、すく、すかす	clear	透
透明	とうめい	transparent	62 g
明	メイ、ミョウ、あかるい、	clear, bright	62 g
踏	トウ、ふむ、ふまえる	tread, step on	踏
踏み込む	ふみこむ	step into	62 g
込	こむ、こめる	be crowded	62 g
逃	トウ、にげる、にがす	escape, evade	逃
逃げ道	にげみち	escape route	62 g
道	ドウ、トウ、みち	way, road	62 g

🜚	働	導	闘
63 a	♎	♉	♎

Labor Takes the Lead in the Fight.

働	ドウ、はたらく	work	働
労働者	ろうどうしゃ	labourer	63 a
労	ロウ	labor, toil	63 a
導	ドウ、みちびく	guide, lead	導
指導	しどう	guidance	63 a
指	シ、ゆび、さす	finger, point	63 a
闘	トウ、たたかう	fight	闘
闘志	とうし	fighting spirit	63 a
志	シ、こころざす、こころざし	will, intent	63 a

🜚	洞	童	憧
63 b	♎	♉	♎

Cave Children Admire cave persons.

洞	ドウ、ほら	cave, penetrate	洞
空洞	くうどう	cavern, cavity	63 b
空	クウ、そら、あく	sky, empty	63 b
童	ドウ、わらべ	child	童
児童	じどう	children	63 b
児	ジ、ニ	child	63 b
憧	ショウ、ドウ、あこがれる	yearn after; long for	憧
憧憬	しょうけい;どうけい	longing; aspiration	63 b
憬	ケイ あこがれる	yearn for; admire	63 b

🜚	読	届	栃
63 c	♎	♉	♎

Readers Reported on Chestnut Mochi Cake.

読	ドク、トク、トウ、よむ	read	読
読者	どくしゃ	reader	63 c
者	シャ、もの	person	63 c
届	とどける、とどく	deliver, report	届
届け出る	とどけでる	notify	63 c
出	シュツ、スイ、でる	emerge, put out	63 c
栃	レイ、とち	horse chestnut	栃
栃餅	とちもち	mochi cake	63 c
餅	ヘイ、もち	mochi rice cake	63 c

♎	曇	頓	奈
63 d	♎	♉	♎

Drifting Clouds in an Orderly Hell.

曇	ドン、くもる	to cloud, dim	曇
曇り勝ち	くもりがち	cloudy	63 d
勝	ショウ、かつ、まさる	win, surpass	63 d
頓	トン、とみに	suddenly	頓
整頓	せいとん	put in order	63 d
整	セイ、ととのえる	arrange	63 d
奈	ナ、いかん	nara; what?	奈
奈落	ならく	Naraka; Hell	63 d
落	ラク、おちる、おとす	fall, drop	63 d

♎	謎	鍋	軟
63 e	♎	♉	♎

The Enigma of the Cauldron calling the kettle Soft.

謎	メイ、なぞ	puzzle; enigma	謎
謎解き	なぞとき	solution of a riddle	63 e
解	カイ、ゲ、とく、とかす	explain, solve	63 e
鍋	カ、なべ	pot; pan; kettle	鍋
大鍋	おおなべ	cauldron	63 e

大	ダイ、タイ、おおきい	big	63 e
軟	ナン、やわらかい	soft	軟
軟弱	なんじゃく	weakness	63 e
弱	ジャク、よわい、よわる	weak	63 e

☿	尼	乳	虹
63 f	♎	♉	♎

This Convent's Dairy Industry produced Rainbow-Coloured cream.

尼	ニ、あま	nun, priestess	尼
尼寺	あまでら	convent (bikuni)	63 f
寺	ジ、てら	temple	63 f
乳	ニュウ、ちち、ち	breasts, milk	乳
乳業	にゅうぎょう	dairy industry	63 f
業	ギョウ、ゴウ、わざ	profession, deed, karma	63 f
虹	コウ、にじ	rainbow	虹
虹色	にじいろ	rainbow-coloured	63 f
色	ショク、シキ、いろ	colour, sensuality	63 f

☿	如	猫	任
63 g	♎	♉	♎

A Competent Cat was Appointed.

如	ジョ、ニョ	similar, equal	如
如才ない	じょさいない	adroit; clever	63 g
才	サイ	talent, year of age	63 g
猫	ビョウ、ねこ	cat	猫
愛猫	あいびょう	pet cat	63 g
愛	アイ	love	63 g
任	ニン、まかせる、まかす	duty, entrust	任
任命	にんめい	appointment	63 g
命	メイ、ミョウ、いのち	life, order	63 g

	57	58	59	60	61	62	63
a	潜水	挿絵	多忙な	遅咲き	追放	宮殿	労働者
	浅薄	素早い	唾棄	拉致	津波	登山	指導
	色染め	掃除機	対応	建築	椎骨	音吐	闘志
b	推薦	紛争	戴白	仲介	生爪	賭場	空洞
	煎餅	痩身	両替え	沖縄	漬物	首都	児童
	羨望	巣立つ	忍耐	竹束	潰瘍	努力賞	憧憬
c	鮮明	変装	奪回	著者	鶴首	凍結	読者
	詮索	青草	濁音	注射	低落	怒鳴る	届け出る
	銭湯	海藻	貸し金	真昼	釣り場	刀刃	栃餅
d	狙撃	大騒ぎ	誰某	彫刻	程度	唐本	曇り勝ち
	修繕	増大	嘆息	特徴	堤防	半島	整頓
	疎外	霜害	担当	懲罰	引締め	哀悼	奈落
e	組合	貯蔵	破綻	潮流	摘発	一等	謎解き
	阻喪	贈賄	短所	朝廷	諦観	桃色	大鍋
	遡行	憎悪	冷淡	挑戦	敵意	病棟	軟弱
f	創造	捕捉	暖炉	眺望	水滴	筒形	尼寺
	双方	満足	男優	超人	溺愛	豆腐	乳業
	倉荷	束の間	花壇	聴心器	補填	解答	虹色
g	妄想	手続き	知合い	沈黙	添乗	透明	如才ない
	爽快	他人	値段	跳ね返る	貼付	踏み込む	愛猫
	伴奏	子孫	用水池	進捗	運転	逃げ道	任命

CHAPTER 10
Weeks 64 – 70

	燃	捻	粘
64 a	♎	♉	♎

For Burns and Sprains use Sticky sludge.

燃	ネン、もえる、もやす、もす	burn	燃
燃焼	ねんしょう	combustion	64 a
焼	ショウ、やく、やける	burn, roast	64 a
捻	ネン、ねじる、ひねる	twirl; twist; play	捻
捻挫	ねんざ	sprain	64 a
座	ザ、すわる	seat, sit, gather	64 a
粘	ネン、ねばる	sticky, glutinous	粘
粘着	ねんちゃく	adhesion	64 a
着	チャク、ジャク、きる	arrive, wear	64 a

	濃	悩	納
64 b	♎	♉	♎

Intensely Painful Tax Payments.

濃	ノウ、こい	thick, deep, rich	濃
濃厚の	のうこうの	rich, intense	64 b
厚	コウ、あつい	thick, kind	64 b
悩	ノウ、なやむ	worry, distress, tease	悩
苦悩	くのう	distress	64 b
苦	ク、くるしい	painful, bitter	64 b
納	ノウ、ナッ、おさめる	obtain, store, supply	納
納税	のうぜい	tax payment	64 b
税	ゼイ	tax, tithe	64 b

	杯	廃	敗
64 c	♎	♉	♎

Raise a Cup to the Abolition of Defeat.

杯	ハイ、さかずき	winecup, cup(ful)	杯
玉杯	ぎょくはい	jade cup	64 c
玉	ギョク、たま	ball, sphere, coin	64 c
廃	ハイ、すたれる、すたる	abandon(ed), obsolete	廃
廃止	はいし	abolition	64 c
止	シ、とまる、とめる	stop	64 c
敗	ハイ、やぶれる	defeat	敗
敗北	はいぼく	defeat	64 c
北	ホク、きた	north, flee	64 c

| ♂ | 培 | 背 | 唄 |
| 64 d | ♎ | ♉ | ♎ |

Cultivate a Defiant Epic Song.

培	バイ、つちかう	cultivate, grow	培
培養	ばいよう	cultivation	64 d
養	ヨウ、やしなう	rear, support	64 d
背	ハイ、せ、せい、そむく	back, stature, defy	背
背負	せおう	carry on one's back	64 d
負	フ、まける、おう	defeat, bear	64 d
唄	バイ、うた	sing	唄
長唄	ながうた	epic Japanese song	64 d
長	チョウ、ながい	long, senior	64 d

| ♂ | 拍 | 剥 | 梅 |
| 64 e | ♎ | ♉ | ♎ |

Applause for Fading Plum Blossoms.

拍	ハク-ヒョウ	beat, tap, clap	拍
拍手	はくしゅ	hand clapping	64 e
手	シュ、て、た	hand	64 e
剥	ハク、ホク、へぐ、むく	come off; peel; fade	剥
剥奪	はくだつ	divest of	64 e

奪	ダツ、うば-う	snatch, captivate	64 e
梅	バイ、うめ	plum (fertility)	梅
梅花	ばいか	plum blossom	64 e
花	カ、はな	flower, blossom	64 e

☿ 64 f	縛 ♎	麦 ♉	箸 ♎

Bind the Wheat and Sheathe the Chopsticks.

縛	バク、しばる	bind	縛
縛り首	しばりくび	hanging	64 f
首	シュ、くび	head, neck, chief	64 f
麦	バク、むぎ	wheat, barley	麦
麦粉	むぎこ	wheat flour	64 f
粉	フン、こ、こな	powder	64 f
箸	チョ、はし	chopsticks	箸
箸紙	はしがみ	paper sheath for chopsticks	64 f
紙	シ、かみ	paper	64 f

☿ 64 g	抜 ♎	畑 ♉	鉢 ♎

Omitting the Salesfield of Headbands.

抜	バツ、ぬく、ぬける	pluck, extract, miss	抜
手抜かり	てぬかり	omission	64 g
手	シュ、て、た	hand	64 g
畑	はた、はたけ	field	畑
営業畑	えいぎょうばたけ	sales field	64 g
営	エイ、いとなむ	conduct, barracks	64 g
業	ギョウ、ゴウ、わざ	profession, deed	64 g
鉢	ハチ、ハツ	bowl, pot, skull	鉢
鉢巻	はちまき	headband	64 g
巻	カン、まく、まき	roll, reel, volume	64 g

🎵	汎	煩	帆
65 a	♎	♉	♎

Philantrophic and Fastidious Sailing.

汎	ハン、う-かぶ、ひろい	pan-	汎
汎愛	はんあい	philanthropy	65 a
愛	アイ	love	65 a
煩	ハン、ボン、わずらう	trouble, pain, torment	煩
煩型	うるさがた	fastidiousness	65 a
型	ケイ、かた	type, model, mould	65 a
帆	ハン、ほ	sail	帆
帆走	はんそう	sailing	65 a
走	ソウ、はしる	run	65 a

🎵	飯	卑	彼
65 b	♎	♉	♎

Insignificant Iniquity on the Other Shore.

飯	ハン、めし	cooked, rice, food	飯
朝飯前	あさめしまえ	trivial matter; piece of cake	65 b
朝	チョウ、あさ	court, morning	65 b
前	ゼン、まえ	before, front	65 b
卑	ヒ、いやしい	lowly, mean, despise	卑
卑劣	ひれつ	baseness	65 b
劣	レツ、おとる	be inferior	65 b
彼	ヒ、かれ、かの	he, that, distant goal	彼
彼岸	ひがん	equinox, other shore, goal	65 b
岸	ガン、きし	bank, shore	65 b

🎵	秘	扉	泌
65 c	♎	♉	♎

Secretive Doors of Secretion.

秘	ヒ、ひめる	(keep) secret	秘
秘蔵	ひぞう	treasure, cherish	65 c
蔵	ゾウ、くら	storehouse, harbor	65 c
扉	ヒ、とびら	door, front page	扉
門扉	もんぴ	doors of a gate	65 c
門	モン、かど	gate, door	65 c
泌	ヒツ、ヒ	flow, secrete	泌
分泌	ぶんぴつ	secretion	65 c
分	ブン、フン、ブ、わける	divide, understand	65 c

	避	飛	費
65 d	♎	♉	♎

There's no Refuge from the Increasing Cost of Living.

避	ヒ、さける	avoid	避
避難	ひなん	taking refuge	65 d
難	ナン、かたい、むずかしい	difficult, trouble	65 d
飛	ヒ、とぶ、とばす	fly	飛
飛躍	ひやく	leap	65 d
躍	ヤク、おどる	leap, dance, rush	65 d
費	ヒ、ついやす、ついえる	spend	費
生活費	せいかつひ	cost of living	65 d
生	セイ、ショウ、いきる	life, birth, grow	65 d
活	カツ	activity, life	65 d

	尾	美	眉
65 e	♎	♉	♎

Tail that Beautiful Eyebrow.

尾	ビ、お	tail	尾
尾行	びこう	shadow; tail	65 e
行	コウ、ギョウ、アン、いく	go, conduct	65 e
美	ビ、うつくしい	beautiful, fine	美

賞美	しょうび	admiration; praise	65 e
賞	ショウ	prize, praise	65 e
眉	ビ、ミ、まゆ	eyebrow	眉
焦眉	しょうび	urgency	65 e
焦	ショウ、こげる、こがす	scorch, fret	65 e

♀	媛	漂	俵
65 f	♎	♉	♎

Talented Women wear Buoyant Bags.

媛	エン、ひめ	beautiful woman; princess	媛
才媛	さいえん	talented woman	65 f
才	サイ	talent, year of age	65 f
漂	ヒョウ、ただよう	float, drift, bob	漂
漂着	ひょうちゃく	drift ashore	65 f
着	チャク、ジャク、きる	arrive, wear	65 f
俵	ヒョウ、たわら	sack, bag	俵
土俵	どひょう	arena, esp. in sumo	65 f
土	ド、ト、つち	earth	65 f

♀	苗	夫	浜
65 g	♎	♉	♎

The Family Name of the Husband means Sandy Beach.

苗	ビョウ、なえ、なわ	seedling, offspring	苗
苗字	みょうじ	family name	65 g
字	ジ、あざ	letter, symbol	65 g
夫	フ、フウ、おっと	husband, man	夫
夫君	ふくん	one's husband	65 g
君	クン、きみ	lord, you mr	65 g
浜	ヒン、はま	beach, shore	浜
砂浜	すなはま	sandy beach	65 g
砂	サ、シャ、すな	sand, gravel, grain	65 g

	富	敷	膚
66 a	♎	♉	♎

A Rich Rug feels luxurious against the Skin.

富	フ、フウ、とむ、とみ	wealth, riches	富
豊富	ほうふ	abundant, rich	66 a
豊	ホウ、ゆたか	abundant, rich	66 a
敷	フ、しく	spread, lay	敷
敷き物	しきもの	rug	66 a
物	ブツ、モツ、もの	thing	66 a
膚	フ はだ	skin	膚
膚着	はだぎ	underwear	66 a
着	チャク、ジャク、きる	arrive, wear	66 a

	武	赴	阜
66 b	♎	♉	♎

Warriors Posted in Gifu.

武	ブ、ム	military, warrior	武
武者	むしゃ	warrior	66 b
者	シャ、もの	person	66 b
赴	フ、おもむく	proceed, go	赴
赴任地	ふにんち	post, posting	66 b
任	ニン、まかせる	duty, entrust	66 b
地	チ、ジ	ground, land	66 b
阜	フ、おか	hill; mound; radical	阜
岐阜	ぎふ	Gifu (city, prefecture)	66 b
岐	キ	fork	66 b

	風	幅	腹
66 c	♎	♉	♎

Angry Taiphoon's Broad Belly.

風	フウ、フ、かぜ、かざ	wind, style	風
台風	たいふう	taiphoon	66 c
台	ダイ、タイ	platform, stand	66 c
幅	フク、はば	width, scroll	幅
横幅	よこはば	breadth	66 c
横	オウ、よこ	side, crossways	66 c
腹	フク、はら	belly, guts	腹
腹立ち	はらだち	anger	66 c
立	リツ、リュウ、たつ、たてる	stand, rise	66 c

| ☃ | 覆 | 沸 | 仏 |
| 66 d | ♎ | ♉ | ♎ |

Bringing Down the Boiling Buddha.

覆	フク、おおう	overturn, cover	覆
転覆	てんぷく	overturn	66 d
転	テン、ころがる	rotate, roll	66 d
沸	フツ、わく、わかす	boil, gush	沸
沸き立つ	わきたつ	seethe	66 d
立	リツ、リュウ、たつ	stand, rise, leave	66 d
仏	ブツ、ほとけ	Buddha, France	仏
仏教	ぶっきょう	Buddhism	66 d
教	キョウ、おしえる	teach	66 d

| ☃ | 公 | 併 | 噴 |
| 66 e | ♎ | ♉ | ♉ |

Fairness is a Jointly Used Fountain.

公	コウ、おおやけ	public, fair, lord	公
公平	こうへい	fairness	66 e
平	ヘイ、ビョウ、たいら、ひら	flat, even, calm	66 e
併	ヘイ、あわせる	unite, join	併
併用	へいよう	joint use	66 e

用	ヨウ、もちいる	use	66 e
噴	フン、ふく	emit, spout	噴
噴水	ふんすい	fountain	66 e
水	スイ、みず	water	66 e

8	壁	閉	米
66 f	♎	♉	♎

A new Wall to Close Off America.

壁	ヘキ、かべ	wall	壁
壁紙	かべがみ	wallpaper	66 f
紙	シ、かみ	paper	66 f
閉	ヘイ、とじる、とざす	close, shut	閉
閉店	へいてん	closing store	66 f
店	テン、みせ	store, premises	66 f
米	ベイ、マイ、こめ	rice, America	米
新米	しんまい	new rice; novice	66 f
新	シン、あたらしい、あらた	new	66 f

8	蔑	片	偏
66 g	♎	♉	♎

Despise the One Hand Prejudice.

蔑	ベツ、ないがしろ、なみする	ignore; despise	蔑
侮蔑	ぶべつ	scorn; disdain	66 g
侮	ブ、あなどる	scorn, despise	66 g
片	ヘン、かた	one side, piece	片
片手	かたて	one hand	66 g
手	シュ、て、た	hand	66 g
偏	ヘン、かたよる	incline, bias	偏
偏見	へんけん	prejudice	66 g
見	ケン、みる、みえる、みせる	look, see, show	66 g

☝	辺	保	穂
67 a	♎	♉	♎

In the Vicinity of Conservative Spear Carriers.

辺	ヘン、あたり、べ	vicinity, boundary	辺
川辺	かわべ	riverside	67 a
川	セン、かわ	river	67 a
保	ホ、たもつ	preserve, maintain	保
保守	ほしゅ	conservatism	67 a
守	シュ、ス、まもる、もり	protect, keep	67 a
穂	スイ、ほ	ear, spear (of grain)	穂
穂先	ほさき	spear	67 a
先	セン、さき	previous, precede, tip	67 a

☝	募	慕	墓
67 b	♎	♉	♎

Recruitment for the Dear Graveyard.

募	ボ、つのる	gather, raise, enlist	募
募集	ぼしゅう	recruitment	67 b
集	シュウ、あつまる、つどう	gather, collect	67 b
慕	ボ、したう	yearn, adore, dear	慕
慕心	ぼしん	yearning	67 b
心	シン、こころ	heart, feelings	67 b
墓	ボ、はか	grave	墓
墓地	ぼち	graveyard	67 b
地	チ、ジ	ground, land	67 b

☝	包	暮	倣
67 c	♎	♉	♎

Wrapping up the morning, the Evening Follows the afternoon.

Kanji Alchemy

包	ホウ、つつむ	wrap, envelop	包
小包み	こづつみ	parcel	67 c
小	ショウ、ちいさい、こ、お	small	67 c
暮	ボ、くれる、くらす	live, sunset, end	暮
夕暮れ	ゆうぐれ	evening	67 c
夕	セキ、ゆう	evening	67 c
倣	ホウ、ならう	imitate, follow	倣
模倣	もほう	imitation	67 c
模	モ、ボ	copy, model	67 c

☝	奉	崩	峰
67 d	♎	♉	♎

An Incredible Landslide on the Main Peak.

奉	ホウ、ブ、たてまつる	offer, respectful	奉
信奉	しんぽう	faith, belief	67 d
信	シン	trust, believe	67 d
崩	ホウ、くずれる、くずす	crumble, collapse	崩
山崩れ	やまくずれ	landslide	67 d
山	サン、やま	mountain	67 d
峰	ホウ、みね	peak, top	峰
主峰	しゅほう	main peak	67 d
主	シュ、ス、ぬし、おも	master, owner	67 d

☝	縫	芳	泡
67 e	♎	♉	♎

Stitching together Fragrant Bubbles.

縫	ホウ、ぬう	sew, stitch	縫
縫針	ぬいばり	sewing needle	67 e
針	シン、はり	needle	67 e
芳	ホウ、かんばしい	fragrant, good, your	芳
芳香	ほうこう	fragrance	67 e

香	コウ、キョウ、かおり	fragrance, incense	67 e
泡	ホウ、あわ	froth, bubble, foam	泡
泡立つ	あわだつ	froth, bubble, foam	67 e
立	リツ、リュウ、たつ	stand, rise, leave	67 e

☞	訪	飽	褒
67 f	♎	♉	♎

When visiting, make sure to sing Untiring Praises.

訪	ホウ、おとずれる、たずねる	visit, inquire	訪
訪問	ほうもん	visit	67 f
問	モン、とう、とい、とん	ask	67 f
飽	ホウ、あきる、あかす	tire, satiate	飽
飽き性	あきしょう	fickleness	67 f
性	セイ、ショウ	nature, sex	67 f
褒	ホウ、ほめる	praise, reward	褒
褒美	ほうび	praise, reward	67 f
美	ビ、うつくしい	beautiful, fine	67 f

☞	亡	傍	坊
67 g	♎	♉	♎

Death was Looking On to the Priest.

亡	ボウ、モウ、ない	die, escape, lose	亡
死亡	しぼう	death	67 g
死	シ、しぬ	death	67 g
傍	ボウ、かたわら	side, beside(s)	傍
傍観	ぼうかん	looking on	67 g
観	カン	watch, observe	67 g
坊	ボウ、ボッ	priest, boy, town	坊
坊主	ぼうず*	priest	67 g
主	シュ、ス、ぬし、おも	master, owner, main	67 g

♂	房	忘	妨
68 a	♎	♉	♎

Within the Room a Nondescript Disturbance was in progress.

房	ボウ、ふさ	room, wife, tuft	房
房中	ぼうちゅう	within a room	68 a
中	チュウ、なか	middle, China	68 a
忘	ボウ、わすれる	forget, leave behind	忘
忘れ勝ち	わすれがち	forgetful	68 a
勝	ショウ、かつ、まさる	win, surpass	68 a
妨	ボウ、さまたげる	hamper, obstruct	妨
妨害	ぼうがい	obstruction	68 a
害	ガイ	harm, damage	68 a

♂	紡	貌	膨
68 b	♎	♉	♎

The Spinning Machine Transformed into a Swollen spider.

紡	ボウ、つむぐ	spin, (yarn)	紡
紡機	ぼうき	spinning machine	68 b
機	キ、はた	loom, device	68 b
貌	ボウ、かお、かたち	appearance	貌
変貌	へんぼう	transformation	68 b
変	ヘン、かわる、かえる	change, strange	68 b
膨	ボウ、ふくらむ	swell, expand	膨
火膨れ	ひぶくれ	blister	68 b
火	カ、ひ、ほ	fire	68 b

♂	睦	墨	頬
68 c	♎	♉	♎

Behold the Friendly, Inked Smile.

睦	ボク、むつむ	intimate; friendly	睦
親睦	しんぼく	friendship	68 c
親	シン、おや、したしい	intimate, parent	68 c
墨	ボク、すみ	ink, inkstick	墨
墨絵	すみえ	ink drawing	68 c
絵	カイ、エ	picture	68 c
頬	キョウ、ほお	cheek	頬
頬笑み	ほおえみ	smile	68 c
笑	ショウ、わらう、えむ	laugh, smile	68 c

♂	勃	翻	磨
68 d	♎	♉	♎

Suddenly, many Reprints of Polish Books appeared.

勃	ボツ、にわかに	suddenness	勃
勃発	ぼっぱつ	outbreak	68 d
発	ハツ、ホツ	discharge, start, leave	68 d
翻	ホン、ひるがえる	flap, change	翻
翻印	ほんいん	reprinting; reissuing	68 d
印	イン、しるし	seal, sign, symbol	68 d
磨	マ、みがく	polish, scour, rub	磨
研磨	けんま	grinding	68 d
研	ケン、とぐ	hone, refine	68 d

♂	麻	幕	枕
68 e	♎	♉	♎

Hemp Curtains and Pillows.

麻	マ、あさ	hemp, flax, numb	麻
麻薬	まやく	narcotic	68 e
薬	ヤク、くすり	medicine, drug	68 e
幕	マク、バク	curtain, tent, act	幕
字幕	じまく	subtitle (movie)	68 e

字	ジ、あざ	letter, symbol	68 e
枕	チン、まくら	pillow	枕
枕元	まくらもと	at one's bedside	68 e
元	ゲン、ガン、もと	originally, source	68 e

♂	務	矛	夢
68 f	♎	♉	♎

Doing your Duty at the Tip of a Nightmare.

務	ム、つとめる	(perform) duty	務
義務	ぎむ	duty	68 f
義	ギ	righteousness	68 f
矛	ム、ほこ	halberd, lance, spear	矛
矛先	ほこさき	spearpoint	68 f
先	セン、さき	previous, precede, tip	68 f
夢	ム、ゆめ	dream	夢
悪夢	あくむ	nightmare	68 f
悪	アク、オ、わるい	bad, hate	68 f

♂	迷	冥	霧
68 g	♎	♉	♎

Being Lost in a Dark Morning Mist.

迷	メイ、まよう	be lost, perplexed	迷
低迷	ていめい	hanging low (over)	68 g
低	テイ、ひくい	low	68 g
冥	メイ, ミョウ	dark	冥
冥福	めいふく	happiness in the next world	68 g
福	フク	good fortune	68 g
霧	ム、きり	mist, fog	霧
朝霧	あさぎり	morning mist	68 g
朝	チョウ、あさ	court, morning	68 g

♂	耗	茂	麺
69 a	♎	♉	♎

Natural Decrease of Thickly Growing Noodles.

耗	モウ、コウ	waste, decrease	耗
減耗	げんこう	natural decrease	69 a
減	ゲン、へる、へらす	decrease	69 a
茂	モ、しげる	grow thickly	茂
繁茂	はんも	luxuriant/dense growth	69 a
繁	ハン	profuse, rich, complex	69 a
麺	メン、ベン、むぎこ	noodles; wheat flour	麺
麺類	めんるい	noodles	69 a
類	ルイ	resemble, variety, sort	69 a

♂	戻	弥	冶
69 b	♎	♉	♎

Bringing Back Yayoi Era Metallurgy.

戻	レイ、もどす、もどる	return, rebel	戻
返戻	へんれい	return	69 b
返	ヘン、かえす、かえる	return	69 b
弥	ミ、ビ、いや、あまねし	increasingly	弥
弥生	やよい	Yayoi period	69 b
生	セイ、ショウ、いきる	life, birth, grow	69 b
冶	ヤ、とける	melting; smelting	冶
冶金	やきん	metallurgy	69 b
金	キン、コン、かね、かな	gold, money, metal	69 b

♂	矢	役	訳
69 c	♎	♉	♎

Targeted Military Interpreting.

矢	シ、や	arrow	矢
矢先	やさき	arrowhead; target	69 c
先	セン、さき	previous, tip	69 c
役	ヤク、エキ	role, service, duty	役
兵役	へいえき	military service	69 c
兵	ヘイ、ヒョウ	soldier	69 c
訳	ヤク、わけ	translation, meaning	訳
通訳	つうやく	interpreting	69 c
通	ツウ、ツ、とおる、かよう	pass, commute	69 c

♂	唯	諭	柳
69 d	♎	♉	♎

Rational Instructors prefer Beautiful Eyebrows.

唯	ユイ、イ、ただ	only, prompt	唯
唯理論	ゆいりろん	rationalism	69 d
理	リ	reason, rational	69 d
論	ロン	argument, opinion	69 d
諭	ユ、さとす	instruct, admonish	諭
教諭	きょうゆ	instructor	69 d
教	キョウ、おしえる	teach	69 d
柳	リュウ、やなぎ	willow	柳
柳眉	りゅうび	beautiful eyebrows	69 d
眉	ビ、ミ、まゆ	eyebrow	69 d

♂	湧	友	憂
69 e	♎	♉	♎

Fermenting Friendship and Seething Sorrow.

湧	ユウ、ヨウ、わく	boil; seethe	湧
湧水	ゆうすい	spring water	69 e
水	スイ、みず	water	69 e
友	ユウ、とも	friend	友

友交	ゆうこう	friendship	69 e
交	コウ、まじわる、まじえる	mix, exchange	69 e
憂	ユウ、うれえる、うれい	grief, sorrow	憂
憂愁	ゆうしゅう	grief, gloom	69 e
愁	シュウ、うれえる、うれい	grief, sadness	69 e

♂	雄	由	遊
69 f	♎	♉	♎

Powerful Reasons for Sightseeing.

雄	ユウ、お、おす	male, powerful	雄
雄犬	めすいぬ	male dog	69 f
犬	ケン、いぬ	dog	69 f
由	ユ、ユウ、ユイ、よし	reason, means, way	由
由縁	ゆえん	relationship, reason, way	69 f
縁	エン、ふち	relation(s), ties, fate, edge	69 f
遊	ユウ、ユ、あそぶ	play, relax	遊
遊覧	ゆうらん	sightseeing	69 f
覧	ラン	see, look	69 f

♂	与	誉	預
69 g	♎	♉	♎

Donating Distinctions and Deposits.

与	ヨ、あたえる	give, convey, impart	与
与え主	あたえぬし	giver, donor	69 g
主	シュ、ス、ぬし、おも	master, owner, main	69 g
誉	ヨ、ほまれ	honor, fame, praise	誉
名誉	めいよ	honour; prestige	69 g
名	メイ、ミョウ、な	name, fame	69 g
預	ヨ、あずける	deposit, look after	預
預金	よきん	deposit	69 g
金	キン、コン、かね、かな	gold, money, metal	69 g

	揚	揺	溶
70 a	♎	♉	♎

Fried Food and Shakes Dissolve the body.

揚	ヨウ、あげる、あがる	raise, fry	揚
揚げ物	あげもの	fried food	70 a
物	ブツ、モツ、もの	thing	70 a
揺	ヨウ、ゆれる、ゆる	shake, swing	揺
揺動	ようどう	shaking	70 a
動	ドウ、うごく、うごかす	move	70 a
溶	ヨウ、とける、とかす、とく	melt, dissolve	溶
溶解	ようかい	melt, dissolve	70 a
解	カイ、ゲ、とく、とかす	explain, solve	70 a

	抑	謡	踊
70 b	♎	♉	♎

Suppression of Folk Singing Dancing Girls.

抑	ヨク、おさえる	restrain, press down	抑
抑圧	よくあつ	suppression	70 b
圧	アツ	pressure	70 b
謡	ヨウ、うたい、うたう	noh chant, song	謡
民謡	みんよう	folksong	70 b
民	ミン、たみ	people, populace	70 b
踊	ヨウ、おどる、おどり	dance, leap, double	踊
踊り子	おどりこ	dancing girl	70 b
子	シ、ス、こ	child	70 b

	浴	沃	翼
70 c	♎	♉	♎

Bathing with a Fertile Pterodactyl.

浴	ヨク、あびる、あびせる	bathe	浴
水浴び	みずあび	bathing	70 c
水	スイ、みず	water	70 c
沃	ヨウ、ヨク、オク、そそぐ	fertility	沃
肥沃	ひよく	fertile	70 c
肥	ヒ、こえる、こえ、こやす	fatten, enrich	70 c
翼	ヨク、つばさ	wing	翼
翼竜	よくりゅう	pterodactyl	70 c
竜	リュウ、たつ	dragon	70 c

♎	落	裸	頼
70 d	♎	♉	♎

Struck by Lightning, the Nudist had one final Request.

落	ラク、おちる、おとす	fall, drop	落
落雷	らくらい	be struck by lightning	70 d
雷	ライ、かみなり	thunder	70 d
裸	ラ、はだか	naked, bare	裸
裸身	らしん	nudity	70 d
身	シン、み	body	70 d
頼	ライ、たのむ、たよる	request, rely	頼
依頼	いらい	request	70 d
依	イ、エ	depend, as is	70 d

♎	絡	嵐	藍
70 e	♎	♉	♎

Contact Stormy Indigo.

絡	ラク、からむ、からまる	entwine, connect	絡
連絡	れんらく	contact	70 e
連	レン、つらなる、つらねる	accompany, row	70 e
嵐	ラン、あらし	storm	嵐
大嵐	おおあらし	raging storm	70 e

大	ダイ、タイ、おおきい	big	70 e
藍	ラン、あい	indigo	藍
出藍	しゅつらん	outshining a teacher	70 e
出	シュツ、スイ、でる、だす	emerge, put out	70 e

⊙€	梨	裏	履
70 f	♎	♉	♎

Harvesting Pears is at the Back of my Personal History.

梨	リ、なし	pear tree	梨
梨狩り	なしがり	harvesting pears	70 f
狩	シュ、かる、かり	hunt	70 f
裏	リ、うら	reverse, side, rear	裏
裏面	りめん	inside, back	70 f
面	メン、おも、おもて	face, aspect, mask	70 f
履	リ、はく	wear (feet), walk, act	履
履歴	りれき	personal history	70 f
歴	レキ	history	70 f

⊙€	律	留	粒
70 g	♎	♉	♎

Legal Caretakers protect their Particles.

律	リツ、リチ	law, control	律
法律	ほうりつ	law	70 g
法	ホウ、ハッ、ホッ	law	70 g
留	リュウ、ル、とめる	stop, fasten	留
留守番	るすばん	caretaker	70 g
守	シュ、ス、まもる、もり	protect, keep	70 g
番	バン	turn, number, guard	70 g
粒	リュウ、つぶ	grain, particle	粒
粒子	りゅうし	particle	70 g
子	シ、ス、こ	child	70 g

	64	65	66	67	68	69	70
a	燃焼	汎愛	豊富	川辺	房中	減耗	揚げ物
	捻挫	煩型	敷き物	保守	忘れ勝ち	繁茂	揺動
	粘着	帆走	膚着	穂先	妨害	麺類	溶解
b	濃厚の	朝飯前	武者	募集	紡機	返戻	抑圧
	苦悩	卑劣	赴任地	慕心	変貌	弥生	民謡
	納税	彼岸	岐阜	墓地	火膨れ	冶金	踊り子
c	玉杯	秘蔵	台風	小包み	親睦	矢先	水浴び
	廃止	門扉	横幅	夕暮れ	墨絵	兵役	肥沃
	敗北	分泌	腹立ち	模倣	頬笑み	通訳	翼竜
d	培養	避難	転覆	信奉	勃発	唯理論	落雷
	背負	飛躍	沸き立つ	山崩れ	翻印	教諭	裸身
	長唄	生活費	仏教	主峰	研磨	柳眉	依頼
e	拍手	尾行	公平	縫針	麻薬	湧水	連絡
	剥奪	賞美	併用	芳香	字幕	友交	大嵐
	梅花	焦眉	噴水	泡立つ	枕元	憂愁	出藍
f	縛り首	才媛	壁紙	訪問	義務	雄犬	梨狩り
	麦粉	漂着	閉店	飽き性	矛先	由縁	裏面
	箸紙	土俵	新米	褒美	悪夢	遊覧	履歴
g	手抜かり	苗字	侮蔑	死亡	低迷	与え主	法律
	営業畑	夫君	片手	傍観	冥福	名誉	留守番
	鉢巻	砂浜	偏見	坊主	朝霧	預金	粒子

CHAPTER 11
Weeks 71 – 73

☿		瞭		旅		涼	
71 a		♎		♉		♎	

Clear Journey to a Cool destination.

瞭	リョウ、あきらか	clear	瞭
明瞭	めいりょう	clarity	71 a
明	メイ、ミョウ、あかるい	clear, bright	71 a
旅	リョ、たび	journey	旅
旅券	りょけん	passport	71 a
券	ケン	ticket, pass	71 a
涼	リョウ、すずしい、すずむ	cool	涼
涼み台	すずみだい	bench	71 a
台	ダイ、タイ	platform, stand	71 a

☿		良		糧		陵	
71 b		♎		♉		♎	

Good Food on the Hill.

良	リョウ、よい	good	良
良心	りょうしん	conscience	71 b
心	シン、こころ	heart, feelings	71 b
糧	リョウ、ロウ、かて	provisions, food	糧
食糧	しょくりょう	provisions	71 b
食	ショク、ジキ、くう、くらう	food, eat	71 b
陵	リョウ、みささぎ	mound	陵
丘陵	きゅうりょう	hill, hillock	71 b
丘	キュウ、おか	hill	71 b

☿		緑		林		臨	
71 c		♎		♉		♎	

Green Forests near the Seaside.

緑	リョク、ロク、みどり	green	緑
緑色	みどりいろ	green	71 c
色	ショク、シキ、いろ	colour, sensuality	71 c
林	リン、はやし	woods, forest	林
林間	りんかん	in the forest	71 c
間	カン、ケン、あいだ、ま	space, gap	71 c
臨	リン、のぞむ	face, verge on, attend	臨
臨海	りんかい	seaside	71 c
海	カイ、うみ	sea	71 c

☿	礼	隣	涙
71 d	♎	♉	♎

Pilgrimage to the Nearby well of Crocodile Tears.

礼	レイ、ライ	courtesy, salute, bow	礼
巡礼	じゅんれい	pilgrim, pilgrimage	71 d
巡	ジュン、めぐる	go around	71 d
隣	リン、とな-る、となり	neighbour, adjoin	隣
隣接	りんせつ	adjacency	71 d
接	セツ、つぐ	contact, join	71 d
涙	ルイ、なみだ	tear	涙
空涙	そらなみだ	crocodile tears	71 d
空	クウ、そら、あく、あける	sky, empty	71 d

☿	麗	鈴	暦
71 e	♎	♉	♎

Beautiful Chimes according the Almanac.

麗	レイ、うるわしい	beautiful	麗
華麗	かれい	splendid, magnificent	71 e
華	カ、ケ、はな	flower, showy, China	71 e
鈴	レイ、リン、すず	bell, chime	鈴
風鈴	ふうりん	wind chime	71 e

風	フウ、フ、かぜ、かざ	wind, style	71 e
暦	レキ、こよみ	calendar, almanac	暦
西暦	せいれき	Anno Domini	71 e
西	セイ、サイ、にし	west	71 e

☿	賂	習	呂
71 f	♎	♉	♎

Bribery Practice for the Spineless.

賂	ロ まいな.い まいなう	bribe	賂
賄賂	わいろ	bribery	71 f
賄	ワイ、まかなう	bribe, provide, board	71 f
習	シュウ、ならう	learn, train	習
練習	れんしゅう	practice	71 f
練	レン、ねる	refine, knead, train	71 f
呂	リョ、ロ	spine; backbone	呂
風呂	ふろ	bath	71 f
風	フウ、フ、かぜ、かざ	wind, style	71 f

☿	弄	朗	遺
71 g	♎	♉	♎

Playful and Cheerful Omissions.

弄	ロウ、ル、いじくる	play with; trifle with	弄
愚弄	ぐろう	mockery; derision; ridicule	71 g
愚	グ、おろか	foolish	71 g
朗	ロウ、ほがらか	clear, fine, cheerful	朗
朗報	ろうほう	good news	71 g
報	ホウ、むくいる	report, reward	71 g
遺	イ、ユイ	leave, bequeath, lose	遺
遺漏	いろう	omission, negligence	71 g
漏	ロウ、もる、もれる	lose	71 g

༄	話	脇	麓
72 a	♎	♉	♎

Sad Stories about Armpits and Feet.

話	ワ、はな-す、はなし	tale, talk	話
哀話	あいわ	sad story	72 a
哀	アイ、あわれ、あわれむ	sorrow, pity	72 a
脇	キョウ、わき	armpit; the other way	脇
小脇	こわき	under one's arm/armpit	72 a
小	ショウ、ちいさい、こ	small	72 a
麓	ロク、ふもと	foot of a mountain	麓
山麓	さんろく	foot of a mountain	72 a
山	サン、やま	mountain	72 a

༄	惑	腕	丼
72 b	♎	♉	♎

In Troubling times, Trusty Types throng to the Tempura tent.

惑	ワク、まどう	be confused	惑
迷惑	めいわく	trouble	72 b
迷	メイ、まよう	be lost, perplexed	72 b
腕	ワン、うで	arm, skill	腕
手腕家	しゅわんか	able individual	72 b
手	シュ、て、た	hand	72 b
家	カ、ケ、いえ、や	house, specialist	72 b
丼	トン、どんぶり	bowl; bowl of food	丼
天丼	てんどん	tempura over a bowl of rice	72 b
天	テン、あめ、あま	heaven, sky	72 b

༄	傲	哺	刹
72 c	♎	♉	♎

Some Snobbish Suckling at the Ancient Temple.

傲	ゴウ、おごる、あなどる	be proud	傲
傲然	ごうぜん	haughty	72 c
然	ゼン、ネン	duly, thus, so, but	72 c
哺	ホ、はぐくむ、ふくむ	nurse; suckle	哺
哺育	ほいく	suckling; nursing	72 c
育	イク、そだつ、そだてる	raise, educate	72 c
刹	サツ、セツ	temple	刹
古刹	こさつ	ancient temple	72 c
古	コ、ふるい、ふるす	old	72 c

𝍒	嘲	喩	浦
72 d	♎	♉	♎

Hovering Insult like a Metaphorical Bay Breeze.

嘲	チョウ、トウ、あざりる	ridicule; insult	嘲
自嘲	じちょう	self derision	72 d
自	ジ、シ、みずから	self	72 d
喩	ユ、たとえる、さとす	metaphor	喩
比喩	ひゆ	metaphor	72 d
比	ヒ、くらべる	compare, ratio	72 d
浦	ホ、うら	coast, inlet, bay	浦
浦風	うらかぜ	bay breeze	72 d
風	フウ、フ、かぜ、かざ	wind, style	72 d

𝍒	毀	恣	惧
72 e	♎	♉	♎

Censorious Abritary Apprehension.

毀	キ、こぼつ、やぶる	break; destroy	毀
毀損	きそん	damage; defamation	72 e
損	ソン、そこなう、そこねる	loss, spoil, miss	72 e
恣	シ、ほしいまま	selfish; arbitrary	恣

恣意	しい	selfishness	72 e
意	イ	mind, thought, will	72 e
惧	ク、おそ.れる	fear; dread	惧
危惧	きぐ	apprehension	72 e
危	キ、あぶない、あやうい	dangerous	72 e

㊂	慄	摯	鬱
72 f	♎	♉	♎

Dreadful and Serious Gloom.

慄	リツ、ふるえる、おそ.れる	fear	慄
慄然	りつぜん	in horror	72 f
然	ゼン、ネン	duly, thus, so, but	72 f
摯	シ、いたる	gift; seriousness	摯
真摯	しんし	earnest	72 f
真	シン、ま	true, quintessence	72 f
鬱	ウツ、うっする、ふさぐ	gloom; depression	鬱
憂鬱	ゆううつ	depression	72 f
憂	ユウ、うれえる、うれい	grief, sorrow	72 f

㊂	箋	緻	籠
72 g	♎	♉	♎

Prescriptions for Delicate Baskets.

箋	セン、ふだ	paper; label; letter	箋
処方箋	しょほうせん	prescription for medicine	72 g
処	ショ	deal with, place	72 g
方	ホウ、かた	side, way, direction	72 g
緻	チ、こまかい	fine (i.e. not coarse)	緻
緻密	ちみつ	minute; fine; delicate	72 g
密	ミツ	dense, secret	72 g
籠	ロウ、ル、かご、	basket; devote oneself	籠
籠城	ろうじょう	under siege	72 g

城	ジョウ、しろ	castle	72 g

⌒	羞	訃	諧
73 a	♎	♉	♎

Contrite Obituary in 17 Syllables.

羞	シュウ、はじる、すすめる	feel ashamed	羞
羞恥	しゅうち	feel ashamed	73 a
恥	チ、はじる、はじらう	shame	73 a
訃	フ、しらせ	obituary	訃
訃報	ふほう	news of a death	73 a
報	ホウ、むくいる	report, reward	73 a
諧	カイ、かなう、やわらぐ	harmony	諧
俳諧	はいかい	haikai, poem 17 syl.	73 a
俳	ハイ	amusement, actor	73 a

⌒	踪	貪	辣
73 b	♎	♉	♎

Disappearance of Greed, Bitter and sweet.

踪	ソウ、ショウ、あと	remains; footprint	踪
失踪	しっそう	disappearance	73 b
失	シツ、うしなう	lose	73 b
貪	タン、トン、むさぼる	covet; indulge in	貪
貪欲	どんよく	greed	73 b
欲	ヨク、ほっする、ほしい	greed, desire	73 b
辣	ラツ、からい	bitter	辣
辛辣	しんらつ	bitter; sharp	73 b
辛	シン、からい	sharp, bitter	73 b

	71	72	73				
a	明瞭	哀話	羞恥				
	旅券	小脇	訃報				
	涼み台	山麓	俳諧				
b	良心	迷惑	失踪				
	食糧	手腕家	貪欲				
	丘陵	天丼	辛辣				
c	緑色	傲然					
	林間	哺育					
	臨海	古刹					
d	巡礼	自嘲					
	隣接	比喩					
	空涙	浦風					
e	華麗	毀損					
	風鈴	恣意					
	西暦	危惧					
f	賄賂	慄然					
	練習	真摯					
	風呂	憂鬱					
g	愚弄	処方箋					
	朗報	緻密					
	遺漏	籠城					

One Character One Reading Word-list

		1		2		3		4		5
a	ア	亜	イン	員	オク	憶	ガイ	害	かつ	且
	アイ	挨	イン	韻	オツ	乙	カイ	貝	かぶ	株
	アイ	愛	イン	姻	オン	恩	ガイ	涯	かる	刈
b	アツ	圧	ウ	宇	カ	貨	ガイ	劾	カン	韓
	あつかう	扱	エイ	英	カ	蚊	ガイ	該	カン	看
	アン	案	エイ	衛	カ	科	ガイ	慨	カン	寛
c	イ	椅	エキ	液	カ	可	ガイ	概	カン	簡
	イ	意	エキ	駅	カ	課	かき	垣	カン	閑
	イ	維	エツ	悦	カ	菓	カク	較	カン	感
d	イ	委	エツ	閲	カ	佳	カク	嚇	カン	憾
	イ	医	エツ	謁	カ	禍	カク	拡	カン	完
	イ	胃	エン	演	カ	寡	カク	閣	カン	刊
e	イ	以	エン	宴	ガ	雅	カク	核	カン	款
	イ	緯	エン	援	ガ	賀	カク	穫	カン	館
	イ	尉	オウ	王	ガ	餓	カク	郭	カン	官
f	イ	為	オウ	応	カイ	楷	かた	潟	カン	棺
	イ	威	オウ	翁	カイ	界	カツ	活	カン	漢
	イキ	域	オウ	往	カイ	介	カツ	括	カン	観
g	イチ	壱	オウ	欧	カイ	階	カツ	轄	カン	歓
	いも	芋	オウ	央	カイ	械	カツ	喝	カン	監
	イン	院	オク	億	カイ	拐	カツ	褐	カン	艦

		6		7		8		9		10
a	カン	敢	ギ	儀	キン	禁	ケイ	慶	ゴ	午
	カン	環	ギ	犠	キン	緊	ケイ	渓	コウ	校
	カン	還	ギ	擬	ギン	吟	ゲイ	芸	コウ	郊
b	カン	勘	キク	菊	ギン	銀	ゲキ	劇	コウ	項
	カン	喚	キツ	喫	ク	区	ケツ	傑	コウ	鉱
	カン	缶	キャク	却	ク	句	ケン	憲	コウ	孝
c	ガン	頑	キュウ	給	グ	具	ケン	県	コウ	酵
	キ	軌	キュウ	級	グウ	偶	ケン	検	コウ	稿
	キ	紀	キュウ	旧	グウ	遇	ケン	倹	コウ	衡
d	キ	奇	キュウ	糾	クツ	屈	ケン	件	コウ	洪
	キ	騎	キョ	巨	くる	繰	ケン	券	コウ	康
	キ	揮	キョ	距	クン	訓	ケン	圏	コウ	航
e	キ	棋	キョウ	況	クン	勲	ケン	謙	コウ	坑
	キ	棄	キョウ	協	グン	軍	ケン	顕	コウ	抗
	キ	汽	キョウ	享	グン	郡	ゲン	玄	コウ	侯
f	キ	季	キョウ	凶	ケイ	系	コ	個	コウ	后
	キ	希	キョウ	峡	ケイ	啓	コ	孤	コウ	拘
	キ	規	キョク	局	ケイ	刑	コ	弧	コウ	講
g	キ	岐	キン	斤	ケイ	景	ゴ	碁	コウ	購
	ギ	議	キン	均	ケイ	径	ゴ	護	コウ	恒
	ギ	義	キン	菌	ケイ	警	ゴ	娯	コウ	肯

		11		12		13		14		15
a	コウ	孔	ザイ	材	シ	士	シュ	朱	ジュン	遵
	ゴウ	拷	ザイ	剤	シ	司	シュ	珠	ジュン	循
	ゴウ	号	さき	崎	シ	詞	ジュ	樹	ショ	署
b	ゴウ	剛	サク	柵	シ	嗣	ジュ	儒	ショ	処
	ゴウ	豪	サク	索	シ	誌	ジュ	需	ショ	庶
	コク	克	サク	昨	シ	肢	シュウ	週	ジョ	序
c	コク	酷	サク	錯	シ	祉	シュウ	酬	ジョ	叙
	コク	穀	サク	策	ジ	璽	シュウ	囚	ジョ	徐
	ゴク	獄	さく	咲	ジ	磁	ジュウ	銃	ショウ	晶
d	コン	婚	サツ	拶	ジ	滋	シュク	粛	ショウ	証
	コン	墾	サツ	察	シキ	式	シュク	叔	ショウ	症
	コン	昆	さら	皿	シキ	識	シュク	淑	ショウ	訟
e	コン	紺	サン	賛	ジク	軸	ジュク	塾	ショウ	抄
	サ	佐	サン	算	シツ	疾	ジュツ	術	ショウ	匠
	サ	詐	サン	桟	しば	芝	シュン	俊	ショウ	渉
f	サ	査	ザン	暫	シャ	赦	ジュン	順	ショウ	衝
	サイ	才	シ	視	シャ	舎	ジュン	準	ショウ	硝
	サイ	宰	シ	詩	ジャ	邪	ジュン	准	ショウ	肖
g	サイ	債	シ	師	シャク	爵	ジュン	純	ショウ	章
	サイ	栽	シ	史	シャク	尺	ジュン	旬	ショウ	彰
	サイ	斎	シ	資	シャク	釈	ジュン	殉	ショウ	祥

		16		17		18		19		20
a	ショウ	粧	シン	紳	セキ	析	ソ	租	ダ	駄
	ショウ	昭	シン	審	セキ	席	ソ	措	ダ	堕
	ショウ	紹	シン	信	セキ	籍	ソ	塑	ダ	惰
b	ショウ	賞	ジン	迅	セキ	績	ソウ	壮	ダ	妥
	ショウ	尚	スイ	帥	セキ	斥	ソウ	荘	タイ	胎
	ショウ	掌	スイ	睡	セキ	隻	ソウ	総	タイ	泰
c	ショウ	称	ズイ	随	セツ	摂	ソウ	層	タイ	隊
	ショウ	将	ズイ	髄	セツ	窃	ソウ	僧	タイ	態
	ショウ	奨	スウ	枢	セン	腺	ソウ	燥	タイ	逮
d	ショウ	礁	スウ	崇	セン	仙	ソウ	曹	ダイ	第
	ジョウ	錠	すぎ	杉	セン	線	ソウ	槽	ダイ	題
	ジョウ	剰	スン	寸	セン	旋	ゾウ	像	たき	滝
e	ジョウ	浄	せ	瀬	セン	栓	ゾウ	臓	タク	拓
	ジョウ	条	ゼ	是	セン	遷	ソク	即	タク	濯
	ジョウ	状	セイ	牲	セン	践	ソク	則	タク	択
f	ジョウ	冗	セイ	征	セン	繊	ゾク	俗	タク	宅
	ジョウ	壌	セイ	聖	セン	宣	ゾク	族	タク	託
	ジョウ	嬢	セイ	制	ゼン	膳	ゾク	属	タク	卓
g	ショク	嘱	セイ	製	ゼン	漸	ゾク	賊	ダク	諾
	ショク	職	セイ	斉	ゼン	禅	ソツ	卒	ただし	但
	シン	芯	ゼイ	税	ソ	祖	タ	汰	タツ	達

		21		22		23		24		25
a	たな	棚	チョウ	庁	テイ	帝	トウ	党	ネイ	寧
	タン	単	チョウ	腸	テキ	適	トウ	糖	ネン	念
	タン	誕	チョウ	帳	テツ	鉄	トウ	陶	ノウ	農
b	タン	胆	チョク	勅	テツ	迭	ドウ	銅	ノウ	能
	タン	丹	チン	朕	テツ	哲	ドウ	胴	ノウ	脳
	ダン	談	チン	賃	テツ	徹	ドウ	堂	ハ	把
c	ダン	段	チン	陳	テツ	撤	とうげ	峠	ハ	派
	チ	痴	ツイ	墜	テン	点	トク	篤	ハ	覇
	チ	稚	つか	塚	テン	典	トク	特	バ	婆
d	チク	逐	つぼ	坪	テン	展	トク	徳	ハイ	肺
	チク	畜	テイ	訂	デン	電	トク	匿	ハイ	俳
	チツ	窒	テイ	偵	ト	斗	トク	督	ハイ	排
e	チツ	秩	テイ	貞	ト	徒	ドク	毒	ハイ	輩
	チャク	嫡	テイ	抵	ト	途	トツ	凸	バイ	倍
	チュウ	酎	テイ	邸	ド	奴	トン	屯	バイ	賠
f	チュウ	忠	テイ	逓	トウ	塔	ナ	那	バイ	陪
	チュウ	衷	テイ	廷	トウ	搭	ニ	弐	バイ	媒
	チュウ	駐	テイ	艇	トウ	到	におう	匂	ハク	伯
g	チュウ	宙	テイ	呈	トウ	痘	ニク	肉	ハク	舶
	チュウ	抽	テイ	停	トウ	謄	ニョウ	尿	バク	漠
	チョ	貯	テイ	亭	トウ	騰	ニン	妊	バク	爆

		26		27		28		29
a	はこ	箱	ヒ	批	フ	譜	ホウ	俸
	はだ	肌	ヒ	罷	ブ	部	ボウ	肪
	バツ	伐	ヒ	碑	フク	服	ボウ	剖
b	バツ	閥	ビ	微	フク	福	ボウ	貿
	ハン	班	ひめ	姫	フク	副	ボウ	棒
	ハン	繁	ヒャク	百	フク	復	ボウ	某
c	ハン	藩	ヒョウ	評	ヘイ	丙	ボウ	帽
	ハン	畔	ヒョウ	標	フン	雰	ボク	朴
	ハン	販	ヒョウ	票	フン	墳	ボク	僕
d	ハン	範	ビョウ	秒	ヘイ	弊	ボク	撲
	ハン	版	ヒン	頻	ヘイ	陛	ボツ	没
	ハン	頒	ヒン	賓	ヘイ	幣	ほり	堀
e	ハン	搬	ビン	敏	ベン	弁	ホン	奔
	ハン	般	ビン	瓶	ヘイ	塀	ボン	盆
	バン	番	フ	婦	ヘン	遍	マ	摩
f	バン	晩	フ	府	ボ	簿	マ	魔
	バン	蛮	フ	符	ベン	勉	マイ	毎
	バン	盤	フ	附	ホ	舗	マイ	枚
g	ヒ	妃	フ	扶	ホウ	邦	マク	膜
	ヒ	披	フ	賦	ホウ	砲	また	又
	ヒ	非	フ	普	ホウ	胞	マツ	抹

		30		31		32		33
a	マン	慢	ユウ	幽	リク	陸	レイ	齢
	マン	漫	ユウ	郵	リャク	略	レイ	隷
	ミ	未	ユウ	猶	リュウ	隆	レキ	歴
b	ミ	魅	ユウ	融	リュウ	硫	レツ	列
	みさき	岬	ヨ	予	リョ	慮	レツ	烈
	ミツ	蜜	ヨウ	陽	リョ	虜	レン	錬
c	ミツ	密	ヨウ	曜	リョウ	了	レン	廉
	ミャク	脈	ヨウ	容	リョウ	猟	ロ	炉
	ミョウ	妙	ヨウ	洋	リョウ	料	ロウ	楼
d	むすめ	娘	ヨウ	庸	リョウ	両	ロウ	労
	メイ	銘	ヨウ	擁	リョウ	領	ロウ	浪
	メイ	盟	ヨク	翌	リョウ	僚	ロウ	廊
e	モウ	猛	ラ	羅	リョウ	寮	ロウ	郎
	モウ	盲	ラク	酪	リョウ	療	ロク	録
	モン	紋	ラン	欄	リン	厘	ロン	論
f	ヤク	約	ラン	覧	リン	倫	わく	枠
	ヤク	厄	ラン	濫	ル	瑠	ワン	湾
	ユ	輸	リ	理	ルイ	塁		
g	ユ	愉	リ	吏	ルイ	累		
	ユウ	裕	リ	痢	レイ	令		
	ユウ	悠	リ	璃	レイ	零		

Radicals

1	沿	水；氵	water	29	界	田	rice field	57	館	食；⻟	food
2	位	人；亻	man	30	尽	尸	corpse	58	益	皿	dish
3	拡	手；扌	hand	31	需	雨	rain	59	究	穴	hole
4	議	言；訁	word	32	砂	石	stone	60	書	曰	speak
5	机	木	tree	33	裸	衣	clothing	61	規	見	to see
6	練	糸	thread	34	禍	示；礻	to show	62	駆	馬	horse
7	達	辵；辶	road	35	専	寸	inch	63	岩	山	mountain
8	応	心；忄	heart	36	帥	巾	cloth	64	強	弓	bow
9	台	口	mouth	37	聞	門	gate	65	舶	舟	ship
10	芸	艸；艹	grass	38	疾	疒	sickness	66	衡	行	going
11	宇	宀	crown	39	狂	犬；犭	dog	67	字	子	child
12	鋭	金；釒	metal	40	協	十	cross	68	歴	止	stop
13	院	阜；阝	village	41	回	囗	country	69	犠	牛；牜	cow
14	肢	肉；月	meat	42	転	車	vehicle	70	即	卩	seal
15	垣	土	earth	43	今	人；亻	man	71	翻	羽	wing

16	如	女	woman	44	先	儿	legs	72	群	羊	sheep
17	則	刀; 刂	sword	45	邪	邑; 阝	village	73	旅	方	direction
18	加	力	strength	46	上	一	one	74	殉	歹	death
19	費	貝	shell	47	照	火; 灬	fire	75	蛍	虫	insect
20	箇	竹	bamboo	48	粧	米	rice	76	享	亠	kettle lid
21	早	日	day, sun	49	配	酉	hen, sake	77	亜	二	two
22	積	禾	tree	50	集	隹	old bird	78	乾	乙	2nd in order
23	往	彳	going man	51	収	又	again	79	段	殳	pike
24	広	广	hemp ncl.	52	現	玉; 王	jewel, king	80	壮	士	samurai
25	顔	頁	big shell	53	欲	欠	lacking	81	影	彡	short hair
26	放	支; 攵	chair	54	路	足	leg, foot	82	的	白	white
27	大	大	big	55	共	八	eight	83	少	小	small
28	看	目; 罒	eye	56	干	干	dry, one	84	多	夕	evening

Previously Published

Kanji Alchemy 1 Kindle 978-0-9941964-0-8
Kanji Alchemy 1 Paperback 978-0994196460
Kanji Alchemy 1 Epub 9780994196439
Kanji Alchemy 1 IngramSpark Paperback 9780994196460
Kanji Alchemy 2 Kindle 978-0-9941964-1-5
Kanji Alchemy 2 Paperback 978-0994196477
Kanji Alchemy 2 Epub 9780994196446
Kanji Alchemy 2 IngramSpark Paperback 9780994196477
Kanji Alchemy 3 Kindle 978-0-9941964-2-2
Kanji Alchemy 3 Paperback 978-0994196484
Kanji Alchemy 3 Epub 9780994196453
Kanji Alchemy 3 IngramSpark Paperback 9780994196484
Kanji Alchemy Supplement 1 Kindle ASIN: B082Z51CXQ
Kanji Alchemy Supplement 1 Paperback ASIN: 0648758338
Kanji Alchemy Supplement 2 Kindle ASIN: B082Z5YYXG
Kanji Alchemy Supplement 2 Paperback ASIN: 0648758346
Kanji Alchemy Supplement 3 Kindle ASIN: B082XT33G8
Kanji Alchemy Supplement 3 Paperback ASIN: 0648758354
Kanji Alchemy Back to the Roots Kindle ASIN: B09M6X6YZ7
Kanji Alchemy Back to the Roots Paperback 978-0648758365
Kanji Alchemy Back to the Roots IngramSpark PB 9780648758365
Kanji Alchemy 700 Japanese Charcters
One Reading Kindle 978-0-9941965-0-7
Kanji Alchemy 700 Japanese Characters
One Reading PB 978-0-9941965-1-4
Kanji Alchemy 700 Japanese Characters
One Reading Epub 978-0-9941964-9-1
Kanji Alchemy 700 Japanese Characters
One Reading IngramSpark PB 978-0-9941965-2-1

www.ingramcontent.com/pod-product-compliance
Lightning Source LLC
Chambersburg PA
CBHW070730020526
44118CB00035B/1151